GET PEAK PERFORMANCE EVERY DAY

How to Manage Like a Coach

DR. BEVERLY POTTER

RONIN
Berkeley, CA
www.roninpub.com

GET PEAK PERFORMANCE EVERY DAY

ISBN: 1-57951-071-X

Copyright © 2004 by Beverly A. Potter

Published by
RONIN Publishing, Inc.
PO Box 22900
Oakland, CA 94609
www.roninpub.com

Credits:

Cover design:	Brian Groppe	briangroppe.com
Interior desige	Bevely A. Potter	docpotter.com
Text font:	Venus by Chank	www.chank.com
Cover fonts:	Sodom by Chank	
	Venus by Chank	

Distributed to the trade by Publishers Group West
Printed in the United States of America by United Graphics
Library of Congress Card Number — 2004096983
Printing Number 1

GET PEAK PERFORMANCE EVERY DAY

How to Manage Like a Coach

DR. BEVERLY POTTER

Other Books by Dr. Beverly Potter

OVERCOMING JOB BURNOUT
How to Renew Enthusiasm for Work

FINDING A PATH WITH A HEART
How to Go from Burnout to Bliss

FROM CONFLICT TO COOPERATION
How to Mediate a Dispute

THE WORRYWART'S COMPANION
Twenty-One Ways to Soothe Yourself & Worry Smart

PREVENTING JOB BURNOUT
A Workbook

THE WAY OF THE RONIN
Riding the Waves of Change at Work

HIGH PERFORMANCE GOAL SETTING
Using Intuition to Conceive & Achieve Your Dreams

BRAIN BOOSTERS
Foods & Drugs that Make You Smarter

DRUG TESTING AT WORK
A Guide for Employers

PASSING THE TEST
An Employee's Guide to Drug Testing

THE HEALING MAGIC OF CANNABIS
It's the High that Heals

TURNING AROUND
Keys to Motivation and Productivity

TABLE OF CONTENTS

Part One

Coaching Performance

1

Managing for Peak Performance

MANAGING IS A TOUGH JOB with many responsibilities and little training in how to handle them. You've got to keep a lot of balls in the air while adapting to exploding technology, roller-coasters and meeting deadlines. All while getting the job done and meeting organizational goals. To accomplish this, you must build a team—transform a group of individual contributors into a cohesive and committed work group—who know when to grab the ball and run with it and when to pass it off to another and run interference so that they can score. And you've got to keep that team spirit up in the face of setbacks and economic downturns. At the same time you must treat the people who make up your team as individuals—unique persons with differing capabilities and motivational makeup. Individuals want individual attention. They want to be team players but they also want to shine on their own. You must do all of this while handling multicultural issues and bureaucratic hassles. It is your job to get people performing and to keep them performing at peak levels.

The inherent preferences of organization are clarity, certainty, and perfection. The inherent nature of human relationships involves ambiguity, uncertainty and imperfection. How one honors, balances, and integrates the needs of both is the real trick of management.

—Pascale and Athos

Fortunately, most people want to perform at their peak. So managers and employees are on the same page in this regard. It feels good to excel and self-esteem soars. Productivity is good for the company and good for those who work there. It is a winning bargain when your management methods enlist and enlarge employees.

As a manager, you are responsible for supervision, directing, developing potential, teaching your team members how to perform better on the job and preparing them to move on to new jobs, controlling, evaluating, giving feedback, helping correct substandard performances, motivating, and helping employees generate enthusiasm and commitment to work. Concurrent with handling these complex responsibilities, you have to juggle pressures from above and below in the hierarchy under deadline constraints with a myriad of distractions. The question is how to meet all these demands.

FEUDAL BOSSING RITUALS

MANAGERS HAVE FEW AVAILABLE MODELS for managing excellently. The academic models are just that—too theoretical with too little how-to implementation. Most managers tend to rely on the real life models around them, their corporate culture, and common sense. At one time or another every manager struggles with the dilemma of being too nice or too tough. As you'll see, both approaches are suboptimal.

Nice Guy Boss

FROM AN EARLY AGE, we were taught when asking another
to do something to do so *nicely* by prefacing the
request with "Please" and to acknowledge appreciation with "Thank You." It is considered rude, even
aggressive, to *tell* people what to do, which is viewed
as "being bossy".

These rules work well in polite society. Upon
becoming managers, we must do what we have spent
20, 30 or more years learning not to do—boss people
around and tell them what to do. This conflict makes
it difficult and awkward to comment upon employees'
work, much else to direct then, especially when their
work is not up to par. Wanting employees to see
them as a friend and fearing being unliked becomes a
struggle.

NICE GUYS MAKE BUM BOSSES

WHEN INDUSTRIAL PSYCHOLOGISTS interviewed department
heads in large American corporations they found that
nice guy managers, those who were overly concerned
with being liked and appearing to be the employees'
friend, got less work out of their people and created
lower morale than did the more directive managers
they studied. They found that nice bosses are wishy-
washy and their directives are vague, confusing, even
contradictory.

It's just this type of vagueness that is often cited
as a contributing factor to burnout. For one thing,
vague directives can result in an employee working on
the wrong task, misunderstood expectations and confusion about the scope and nature of one's responsibilities.
In short, completing assignments and achieving excel-
lence are more difficult when being supervised by a nice
guy boss.

Giving feedback is another problem area for nice guy bosses. Just as they resist saying "Do this," nice guys are hesitant to say, "You did this wrong," for fear that if they give negative feedback they won't be liked. Consequently their feedback tends to be confusing or withheld altogether. Because employees don't know how they're doing they are deprived of vital information they need to improve their performance. In short, the nice guy's personal conflict over being a boss creates problems for employees. Nice guy managers tend to forget that implicit in the employment contract is being directed and reviewed. It's expected. In fact, successful completion of work tasks is easier when responsibility, expectations and feedback are clear.

Drill Instructor Boss

LET'S LOOK AT THE DRILL INSTRUCTOR BOSS. Whereas the nice guy says, "Would you please do your work?", the drill instructor boss orders, "Do your work and make it snappy!" Imagine being in a foxhole under fire and hearing, "Oh, by the way, you guys, I think it might be a good idea if you get your heads down." Absurd! You'd be shot. Instead, the commanding officer orders, "Get your heads down," and you obey by dropping down immediately, without questioning.

Compared to nice guy bosses, drill instructors are more effective managers. Employees know what's expected and how their performance stacks up. They get their heads down and the job gets done.

But the drill instructor boss is far from the most effective manager. Drill instructors are not effective in meeting most of the responsibilities we discussed above. The drill instructor model doesn't get partici-pation or gather information; it doesn't develop em-ployee potential, evaluate, or provide feedback; it doesn't promote innovation.

Traditionally, our concepts of leadership, the chain of command, coordination, control, and functional specialization followed the military model. Many managers are guided by beliefs, assumptions, and perceptions about management rooted in the military metaphor. Workers have changed, however. They rebel against the image of being a troop in the trenches. Employees today know more and expect more. Simultaneously, the nature of work has evolved. There are fewer rote tasks and more jobs requiring judgment, initiative, and creativity. Now with the ever-rapid advances in telecommuting technology, employ-ees increasingly work off site under their own direc-tion, further challenging the old approaches to control and coordination.

Coaching Boss

WE NEED A NEW MANAGE-MENT METAPHOR, one that allows for more indi-vidual creativity and participation. Accom-plishing company goals is a team activ-ity and the role of a manager is similar to that of a coach. The single most important task for a coach is to

Being part of a team designing a new program for the company can give people a heightened sense of importance and in-volvement, an experience of creation that punctu-ates the rest of their ongoing work experience.

—Rosebeth Moss Kanter

elicit high performance from the team and its members as individual performers. Coaches do this in two ways: through training—teaching skills needed for peak performance, and through motivation—inspiring players to consistently perform at their peak.

Coaches are both tough and supportive.. They pace the team players in small steps to stretch their abilities. People grow by testing the limits of their abilities against a measure. Coaches create an environment in which stretching ability us rewarding. Coaches teach players how to set specific performance goals to strive for and how to use their last performance as a measure to surpass. Coaches teach achievement motivation—striving for. They encourage the players to exert themselves to stretch to previously undreamed-of heights. Coaches praise progress and give critical feedback that points out areas for improvement.

CREATE A RACE TRACK
AN ARENA OF COMPETITION

Endow work with the characteristics of competitive sports. And the best way to get that spirit into the workplace is to establish some rules of the game and ways for employees to measure themselves. Eliciting peak performance means going up against something or somebody.

Let me give you an example. For years the performance of the Intel facilities maintenance group, which is responsible for keeping our buildings clean and neat, was me-

diocre, and no amount of pressure or inducement seemed to do any good. We then initiated a program in which each building's upkeep was periodically scored by a resident senior manager, dubbed a "building czar" The score was then compared with those given other buildings. The conditions of all of them dramatically improved almost immediately. Nothing else was done; people did not get more money or other rewards. What they did get was a racetrack, an arena of competition. If your work is facilities maintenance, having your building receive top score is a powerful source of motivation.

This is key to the manager's approach and involvement.: he has to see the work as it is seen by the people who do that work every day and create indicators so that his subordinates can watch their "racetrack" take shape.

—Andrew S. Grove

2

Manage Like A Coach

THE SPORTS METAPHOR provides for innovation and adaptability. In any competitive sport, risk is encouraged and periodic failure expected. In business as in sports, one rarely wins all the matches. While winning is a measure of accomplishment, it is achieved by stretching one's abilities is the real objective.

It is one thing to say, "Manage like a coach," and quite another to do so. How do you integrate coaching into a tight

The new leader is a facilitator, not an order giver.

—John Nesbitt

schedule filled with demands, deadlines, and conflicting personalities? What exactly do you do and say? And when? What is involved in creating a race track so that your team can productively compete? To answer these questions we must move from the realm of theory and models to concrete, how to steps.

PROMOTERS OF HIGH MOTIVATION

SETTING GOALS, GIVING FEEDBACK ELICITING PARTICIPATION, and acknowledging good work are the four promoters of high motivation.

GOAL-SETTING

HAVING A GOAL TO STRIVE FOR promotes peak performance, which translates into increased productivity. Industrial psychologists demonstrated the effectiveness of goal-setting in a program conducted with 20 pulpwood-logging operators. Half of the producers were trained in goal-setting and half were not. Each week trainer and producer determined minimum production goals. Using the goal-setting training, the producer converted the goal into cords-per-sawhand-hour and assigned it to the workers who directly controlled that production variable—the sawyers themselves. The sawyers were told that the goal was a minimum standard. They monitored their performance with tally meters. Both control and target producers recorded production, turnover, absenteeism, and injuries for their crews.

Results after 12 weeks revealed that compared with controls, producers who set goals increased their production and decreased their absenteeism significantly.

There was no change in turn over or injury rates. The researchers hypothesized that it was the sense of satisfaction that comes with accomplishing a goal that led to reduction in absenteeism. Work becomes more rewarding and consequently worker attendance increases.

Let's take a closer look at each aspect of this interaction. First, the goals set were clear, specific, and attainable. Goals were stated in terms of workers' tasks. Sawyer goals were set in terms of cords-per-sawhand-hour and producer goals were in terms cords-per-man-hour. The goals clarified for both supervisor and subordinate what they were to get done. By providing specific knowledge about job tasks and priorities, the goals prompted improved performance.

Goals were clear, specific, and attainable.

Goals were stated in terms of workers' tasks.

Improved performance must be rapidly and frequently reinforced if it is to be maintained and if goal-setting is to be established as an ongoing motivator. The data collection and self-monitoring procedures solved this problem. Sawyers recorded how much wood they cut, and producers recorded the collective productivity rates of the sawyers they supervised. In the process of recording, each received immediate *feedback* on performance.

Comparisons between the goal and feedback tend to have two results: When people attain or surpass a goal, they tend to reinforce themselves with positive thoughts—a sense of satisfaction. If they fall short of the goal, their tendency will be to exert more effort to improve performance, provided that positive consequences seem probable—that is, people must see the goal as attainable and believe that they will be rewarded for achieving it.

In this program the goals were determined from an assessment of the harvest area and time studies made under similar conditions. There were no penalties for failure; instead praise was given for attaining the goal. Thus, producers and sawyers alike were likely to have viewed their goals as attainable and were motivated to achieve them. When they did reach the goal, they were reinforced externally with praise and internally with self-reinforcement. In this way, goals prompted improved performance.

Learned to Self-Manage

WE WOULD EXPECT that goal-setting plus self-feedback would promote the learning of self-management—self-directed behavior. The intervention sets the stage for employees to learn to set their own task goals and to acknowledge themselves for reaching them. The supervisor seems to be a critical factor

in this process. The researchers conducted another program with loggers that demonstrated that high-productiv-
ity crews had supervisors who were more accessible and
who gave more training, instruction, and explanation;
whereas crews with inaccessible supervisors had higher
turnover rates. Supervisors can teach subordinates to set
individual task goals and thus reinforce their accomplishment. In other words, in the process of setting goals with
employees, the supervisor probably informally teaches
self-management.

PARTICIPATION

MANAGERS ARE TROUBLESHOOTERS. You are expected to spot
problems, make decisions, and implement solutions, which
requires information about what's going on. Who knows the
nitty-gritty, day-to-day problems of a given job? Those at
the top? No, the person doing the job knows more about
that job, its problems, and potential solutions than does
anyone else. Think about it. Employees are an invaluable
source of information, vital to the survival and profits of
the company. Organizational structure provides for the
flow of information from the top down through the chain
of command. But the challenge for companies is getting
information from the bottom up to the decision makers at
the top.

Participation and gathering information by encouraging
employees to talk about the problems they are experiencing and their ideas for solutions and innovation is needed.
Getting participation is a complex skill. Managers often

Getting participation is a complex skill. attend workshops where they learn the importance of participation. The next day they go back to their staff and say, "All right you guys, I want you all to partici- pate!" What happens? Chances are em- ployees clam up, because *demanding* participation rarely works.

Participative Goal-Setting

WHEN EMPLOYEES PARTICIPATE IN SETTING GOALS, they set higher goals and achieve them more often. In another logger project researchers demonstrated that the nature of the supervisor-subordinate relationship is critical in the success of goal-setting programs. The target of the study was 48 logging crews, half of which were classified as marginal or educationally disadvantaged (workers had educational levels below the ninth grade) and remainder of which were classified as educated (workers with least a high school education).

The intervention was similar to those in the other logger programs. Producers handled goal-setting with the crews in one of three ways: Those who used participative goal-setting re- quired their crew to determine difficult but attainable weekly production goals; those in assigned goal groups set specific goals without consulting their crews; those in control groups urged their crews to do their best (vague goals). Sawyers in goal- setting crews monitored their performance with tally meters.

The results after eight weeks revealed that among the uneducated sawyers, those who participated in goal-setting set higher goals, accomplished their goals more often, and produced more than sawyers in the other groups. This finding supports the principle that in allowing workers to participate in goal-setting, the supervisor actually trains them in goal-setting and reinforces

Those who participated in goal-setting set higher goals, and accomplished their goals more often. improvement. The data from the educated crews showed that there were differences among the three kinds of goal-setting.

Unfortunately, management in the company with the educated crews did not support the program. Consequently, although goals were set, educated crews did not receive "stimulation, counseling, and encouragement." The failure of the program with educated crews emphasizes the significance of the supervisor as well as the importance of top management support.

More Specific Is Better

Most organizational goal-setting programs focus on production goals. To meet production goals, however, workers must complete individual tasks. Completing tasks requires engaging in a series of behaviors, yet goal-setting programs in organizational settings often overlook behavioral-based objectives. Researchers found the behavioral objective approach effective in increasing the productivity of engineers and scientists—provided that they participated in setting the goals. Again the program was similar to those used with the loggers: Thirty-eight managers were trained in goal-setting and 76 subordinate engineers participated in goal-setting or were assigned goals by their managers. Engineers monitored their performance with behavioral checklists. Findings revealed that engineers in both assigned and participative groups were equally committed to their goals and saw them as advantageous, relevant, and potentially satisfying. The main difference was that those who participated set higher goals.

In a second phase of the program, data were collected on engineers and scientists six months after goal-setting. Engineers with specific goals, regardless of whether they were assigned or participative, produced more than those who were urged to do their best (vague goal) or those who had no goals at all (control group).

The more specific the goal, the higher the performance. In other words, the more specific the goal, the higher the performance. As in the case of the loggers, engineers who participated in setting their own goals set more difficult performance goals and produced more.

Let's summarize the outcomes of the goal-setting programs. Most notable is that when combined with feedback, goal-setting resulted in increased levels of productivity. Specificity is important: Specific goals led to more productivity, whereas a vague goal ("do your best") did not. Subordinates' participation in the goal-setting process was a critical variable. Beyond specificity and participation, little is known about the impact of goals on performance. A functional analysis revealed that goals prompt improved behavior, which is then reinforced with feedback.

Participation led to more difficult goals, which were accomplished more often and resulted in higher productivity.

Using Participative Goal-Setting to Teach Self-Management

THE SUPERVISOR PLAYS A CRITICAL ROLE in setting this process in action. When given a vague goal and little supervision, a subordinate is likely to set inappropriate goals (too low or too high). Supervisors can coach subordinates in setting specific, appropriate (difficult but attainable) goals. During this process, subordinates learn how to set goals for themselves. The supervisor can provide positive consequences for improved performance. Once set in motion, self-monitoring provides feedback, which prompts self-reinforcement and additional goal-setting. At this point the supervisor can maintain the process with periodic reinforcement for setting goals, recording data, and improving performance.

The program demonstrated that goals expressed in terms of specific behaviors can be used to improve productivity. Behavioral objectives have many advantages.

ADVANTAGES OF BEHAVIORAL OBJECTIVES

FIRST, task or production goals specify an outcome, but not how much of what behavior is required to accomplish that outcome; behavioral objectives do this.

Second, when subordinates participate in setting their own behavioral objectives, they have an opportunity to learn work performance. They learn to focus on their own behavior and its relationship to outcome. Providing consequences to oneself for performance is another self-management technique. The self-monitoring procedures help maintain a focus on one's own behavior, provide immediate feedback, and prompt self-acknowledgment.

Industrial psychologists evaluated a performance planning and evaluation system for management development employed in a large broad-based international corporation. The premise behind the program was that constant management is important and that an ongoing dialogue between manager and employee at every level of the organization is the basis for such continued development. Three overriding program goals were established: (1) improved on-the-job effectiveness by each employee in his or her present position; (2) self-development of each employee to promote future effectiveness and career growth; and (3) identification of managers who were capable of handling, greater responsibility.

To accomplish these goals, a task force representing each division in the company developed a flexible program that could be tailored to individual needs and circumstances. Top-level commitment and support were demonstrated through publicity statements and the active participation of the president. Fifteen thousand managers were trained in the identification of job responsibilities (outputs expected) and performance planning (setting personal development goals). Five thousand managers of managers were trained in performance evaluation, coaching, and counseling. Once a year, employee and supervisor met for performance planning. During their dialogue, specific aspects of the job were discussed and performance goals were agreed upon and recorded. Periodically the supervisor checked progress, gave feedback, and suggested ways to improve. At the end of the year a formal performance evaluation was made. In this meeting, actual performance was compared with the stated behavioral objectives. Employees discussed with the supervisor how they were doing, and participated in developing a self-development plan for the next year.

There was significant attitude change across the board after only six months of the program. A survey was made of a random sample of over, 4,000 managers, half of whom were using goal-setting and half of whom were not. Users reported that goals were clearer, that they participated more in goal-setting and received more feedback on goal accomplishment. Users also reported having more job autonomy and variety, more work group cohesion, more satisfaction with pay, more promotional opportunities, and less job tension than did nonusers.

The supervisor-employee dialogues provided an opportunity for supervisors to develop and refine their coaching skills.

The supervisor-employee dialogues provided an on-the-job opportunity for supervisors to develop and refine their management skills. This process was repeated at every level of the company. Thus, each manager was constantly involved in self-development activities. On the one hand, each manager had a personal yearly performance plan; on the other hand, each practiced and perfected his or her supervisory skills with subordinates. The locus of this development was the goal-setting and evaluation meeting.

FEEDBACK

FEEDBACK IS INFORMATION TO A WORK UNIT—individual, group, organization—about its performance. Feedback itself is neutral. The way in which the information is dispensed and how it is interpreted by the person receiving the feedback gives it the power to reward or punish. The supervisor who uses feedback to berate a subordinate for substandard performance is translating feedback into a punitive consequence, which is counterproductive and should be avoided. A supervisor who presents feedback in terms of progress towards a goal is translating it into a motivating consequence. Here are some guidelines for effective feedback.

•Feedback Should Be Related to the Goal

WHEN COMBINED WITH GOAL-SETTING, feedback provides guidance and direction so that both manager and subordinates know when they are performing up to standard and they need to improve. Goals and objectives stated in terms of the behaviors needed for achieving them can be assigned or individually negotiated. Likewise, feedback is a particularly useful adjunct to the shaping technique in which small steps of the desired goal behavior are rewarded. Monitoring the feedback quickly tells when the current goal has been reached and when a new objective should be set.

•Give Feedback to the Person Who Controls Performance.

Feedback has the most impact when it is directed to the person or group directly involved. In most cases this would mean the employee and immediate supervisor. When employees are committed to the goal, feedback that indicates improvement can be particularly reinforcing, which tends to foster more improvement. Additionally, feedback tells you when to acknowledge improvement. Feedback is also error-correcting because it points out when additional efforts are necessary to correct declines in performance.

•Collect Feedback on the Appropriate Behavior

If the goal is to increase the quality of word processing, for example, collecting feedback on the quantity of letters and reports produced per day may be counterproductive because it is likely to be an impetus to increase speed at the expense of quality. If quality is a priority, the feedback should be collected on quality of each unit produced rather than on quantity.

•Feedback Should be Timely

Like reinforcement, feedback should be timely. Obviously, an employee can't correct a mistake six months after the fact. The most rapid learning takes place when feedback is immediate and continuous. The best way to shorten the gap between performance and feedback is to have employees collect data on their own performance. The data collected not only provide the employee with immediate information, but can be used as the baseline for evaluating effectiveness of your efforts. In addition, it puts responsibility for monitoring performance on the employee rather than on you. Such self-monitoring can be the first step in teaching self-directed behavior to employees. Finally, self-monitoring can maintain the gains made.

•Stress the Positive, Ignore the Negative

EXPRESS FEEDBACK in terms of how closely it approximates the desired goal. Feedback should be information on the frequency of the desired behavior—for example, number of sales made, length of up time of equipment, number of invoices completed correctly. Information on successes or improvement tends to be more reinforcing than information on failures and setbacks. Further, for reasons not fully understood, behavior tends to change simply as a result of attention. If you pay attention to the behavior you desire, that behavior tends to increase. We all know of cases where a bratty kid who is punished behaviors even more the brat.

•Present Feedback Graphically

A GRAPH IS LIKE A PICTURE—it depicts movement. At the end of each day the data for that day can be recorded on a graph. It is best when employees maintain the graphs because they are powerful motivators. When it makes sense to, post the graph so that others can see the person's progress. In this way an employee's peers can provide reinforcement by commenting on improvement. When the target is a work group, posting of the graph is essential.

3

TASC+ Coaching

*T*ASC+ IS A GUIDE TO MANAGING LIKE A COACH. It is easy to use on the daily playing field where the action is, not just on the sidelines. TASC+ can be integrated into your ongoing minute-to-minute interactions with employees. Special meetings are not required.

TASC+ provides a framework setting goals, giving feedback eliciting participation, and acknowledging good work—the four promoters of high motivation. Let's take a look.

TASC+ stands for *Tell* how performance compares with what's expected; *Ask* for information; *Specify* action or objective; *Check* performance; the plus stands for *Acknowledge* "on TASC" performance.

TASC+ is flexible and lends itself to individualization. TASC+ can be used with employees falling anywhere along the directiveness continuum from traditionally directed to those working autonomously.

TELL

TELL THE EMPLOYEE WHAT'S EXPECTED or the standard to be met. The rule of thumb for tell is best illustrated by Sergeant Friday from the TV classic "Dragnet" in which Friday was famous for saying, "I want the facts ma'am, nothing but the facts!"

Be Specific

Bᴇ sᴘᴇᴄɪꜰɪᴄ ɪɴ ᴅᴇsᴄʀɪʙɪɴɢ ᴏᴜᴛᴄᴏᴍᴇs, such as "a completed design proposal" or "fill out eight forms per hour," or in describing behaviors such as "smile and greet customers when they come to the register."

Avoid being vague such as, " You should be coopera-tive." "Be friendly to customers , or "We expect you to show initiative" The meaning of words like cooperation, friendly, and initiative varies too much to know precisely what is expected or where one stands. In addition, strive to be objective by avoiding judgmental and emotional statements such as, "You look pretty sloppy." Or "This is a half–assed job." Such descriptions convey disapproval but little concrete information about what's wrong. Poorly stated Tells are guaranteed to derail communication by putting people on the defensive.

Be Concise

Dᴏɴ'ᴛ ʀᴀᴍʙʟᴇ, repeat, or go on tangents in which the essen-tial message gets lost in a barrage of verbiage that feels like a harangue. And avoid clouding the issue by justifying, defending or apologizing. Justifying gains little and encour-ages arguments and attacks.

Focus On One Thing

Dᴇsᴄʀɪʙᴇ ᴏɴᴇ sɪᴛᴜᴀᴛɪᴏɴ or one comparison to the standard at a time. Don't piggyback with "and another thing...." Which can overload and come across as harangue. Where there is no comparison performance, simply describe the situation or expectation, following the principle of " Just the facts, Ma'am, nothing but the facts."

Feedback

Tᴇʟʟ ᴘʀᴏᴠɪᴅᴇs A ᴛᴀʀɢᴇᴛ ᴛᴏ sʜᴏᴏᴛ ꜰᴏʀ, a bull's eye to aim at. But a target alone is not enough. There must also be feedback so that employees know where their arrows are hitting. Thus, to be effective when telling employees what is expected, a manager must add how their performance compares to what is expected. "Jason, the standard is for clients to get a callback within 15 minutes. Your callback are averaging 21 minutes." Such a Tell helps the employee to view his performance in perspective.

ASK

THE SINGLE MOST COMMON ERROR MANAGERS MAKE is to jump to conclusions instead of asking for information. It's easy to get into the habit of telling, telling, telling and forget that the employee is a valuable source of information.

Asking is the tool for getting information and eliciting participation. When you ask a question, pressure is put on the employee to answer. This is what's meant by " eliciting participation." By responding thoughtfully to the employee's answer, you actively encourage further participation.

Asking questions is also an ideal tool for developing employee potential. Developing potential means teaching employees skills. The Socratic method— teaching by asking questions—is considered one of the best ways to facilitate learning. For example, if I ask you a question, does it mean I don't know the answer? What is the reason for my asking question? I ask because the question makes you think. In the process you learn and retain.

Ask Open Questions

TO BE EFFECTIVE, however, questions must be well-phrased. Probe with open questions that begin with "what," "when," "where," "how," "who," "in what way," under what conditions," and avoid questions beginning with "why." Why-

Poor and Better ASK

Poor	Better
"Did the machine give you trouble?"	"What happened?" "What caused the trouble?"
"Does the noise bother you?"	"What bothers you about this?"
"Would better directions from me help?"	"What would help?" "How can I help?"
"Are you looking for responsibility?"	"What are you looking for?"
"Do you have any questions?"	"What questions do you have?"
"Do you have any suggestions?"	"What suggestions do you have?"
"Do you think you could keep me informed with a weekly memo?"	"How can you keep me informed?"
"Why are you late?"	"What happened" "What delayed you getting here?"
"Why did you do that?"	"What happened?" "What was the reason for doing that?"
"Do you want to get ahead?"	"What do you want?"
"Are you nervous?"	"How do you feel?"
"You're upset, aren't you?"	"How do you feel?"
"Do you think you can get this done today?"	"What can you do to get this done today?" "When can you get this done?"
"Do you think you can be on time tomorrow?"	"What can you do to get here on time tomorrow?"
"Does the valve need to be replaced, or is it the regulator?"	"What's the problem with this?" "What caused the malfunction?"

questions tend to put employees on the defensive, eliciting justifications and excuses, instead of facts.

Likewise, avoid closed questions that can be answered with yes or no, such as, "Do you...?" "Can't you...?" "Will you...?" Closed questions are insidious because they encourage you to leap to conclusions and talk excessively, which are two communication roadblocks. Closed questions are appropriate for prosecuting but not for gathering good information.

Another danger of closed questions is that they are almost always leading questions that imply the answer you expect. What are bosses looking for when they ask, "Are you looking for responsibility?" They are probably expecting to hear "Responsibility", right? What if the boss asks, "How do you feel about responsibility?" Although this question is open-ended, it is still leading compared to "What are you looking for?", which contains no content that suggests what the boss thinks the person ought to be looking for. Leading questions curtail problem solving by narrowing the focus of discussions to what is suggested in the question. Some examples of poor and better questions are list in the table.

Take your time and don't race through the Ask step. Instead, ask enough questions to get all the information. This is important. And keep an open mind. Consider everything said, otherwise employees will clam up, cutting you off from needed information. Instead, listen and ask more questions. Remember, listening is not agreeing but it is essential for considering and making good decisions.

Use Active Listening

ACT IN SUCH A WAY AS TO COMMUNICATE "I am listening. I want to hear what you have to say." Use body language such as eye contact, nodding, or leaning forward. Don't rifle through papers, or let the phone or others interrupt.

Ask for suggestions. Remember, the person doing the job knows more about what's happening vis-à-vis his or her job than you do. As a coach, your challenge is to get employees to solve problems pertaining to their work. When you stop trying to solve employees' problems for them, a tremendous burden is removed from your shoulders. You don't have to have all the answers! Instead, all you have to do is facilitate employees in finding answers. *So ask for suggestions.*

Avoid Derailment

OF COURSE, NOT EVERY SUGGESTION IS A GOOD ONE. Some may be unfeasible or even off the wall. Generally, there are three situations in which unacceptable suggestions are given. The employee may be trying to sabotage you by deliberately offering an unacceptable suggestion. If you respond with something like "Come on, be serious! I want a suggestion that will work, " You're likely to get the retort "I knew you wouldn't listen, so why bother!" Other times the employee will probably feel foolish and clam up. Finally, the suggestion may actually be a good one and it is you who can't see its creativity! Here the employee probably considers you to be closed minded and even rigid.

How can these pitfalls be avoided? Instead of discounting unfeasible suggestions, ask a question designed to reveal the flaws. "How would that work?" "How would you get that funded?" "How would you get that by JB ?" If the suggestion was meant to sabotage, the bomb is in the saboteur's lap. Naive employees, on the other hand, don't feel put down. Instead, when attempting to answer, they discover what's wrong with the suggestion. When the suggestion is a creative one, the employee has an opportunity to argue its creative aspects, and you can evaluate it without looking old-fashioned or closed-minded

SPECIFY

IN THE *SPECIFY* STEP, information and suggestions gathered during Ask are translated into a plan of action. It is vital that the action be described in specific terms. Indicate who will do what under what conditions and to what extent (how long, how many, how fast, to what degree).

Vaguely stated plans lead to problems of interpretation and accountability. For example, "Try to work harder" applies pressure but doesn't say what is regarded as harder work. Does hard work mean to write long reports, or to put in overtime, or to speak up at meetings? A vague Specify can point the employee in the wrong direction.

Use Small Steps

CONCENTRATE ON SHORT-TERM STEPS to handling the situation or meeting the expectation described in the Tell step. Focus on what will be completed or performed today or this week. Use small, specific steps to help employees pace themselves in accomplishing long-term goals. A side benefit is that in the process of working out the small steps, employees learn how to break distant goals into discrete, doable steps to be taken today. As a result, self-starting and follow-up skills are enhanced.

A well-stated Specify helps accountability. A coach wouldn't say, "Try to run faster." The coach would add a concrete measure to the objective. "This time strive to make the run in 2 minutes 15 seconds." Likewise, "Increase your speed from seven forms completed in an hour to eight," is better than "Work faster this week," because it is easy to determine when the objective has been met.

Here is the step in which you create an arena of competition. Instead of plodding along with no markers of accomplishment, the measure makes the evaluation of progress possible. An objective that is just a small step away encourages stretching. Specifies that have no concrete measure deprive the employee of essential performance feedback. It is much like asking the archer to improve shooting without providing a specific target and not telling him where the last arrow fell. Under such conditions, performance rarely improves and motivation rapidly evaporates. Use quantitative terms because they provide an observable

Describe what is wanted rather than what is wrong. measure of accomplishment. Both you and the employee can tell when performance is "on–TASC."

When a plan of action pertains to a particular behavior or performance, describe it in terms of the doing of specific actions. If a screenwriter, for example, described a character as "acting nervous" director and actor might have conflicting interpretations of how to act the scene. To minimize this problem, scripts describe characters' actions on the *doing level.* "He paced back and forth, frowning and wringing his hands frantically."

Describe the small step specifically enough to give the person a picture of what he is to do. Instead of "be more friendly to customers," say "greet the customers, with a smile as they enter the shop and ask if you may assist them." Describe what is wanted rather than what is wrong. "Don't announce it before checking with me," becomes "check with me before announcing it."

Negotiating the plan and its details with the employees is better than directing them. By doing so you have an opportunity to draw upon the employees' experience and knowledge as well as encouraging their commitment. Additionally, this is your opportunity to teach employees to self-start and take more initiative.

In early use of TASC+, you may assume most of the responsibility for working out the details of Specify. Keep in mind that you are simultaneously teaching the employees how to Specify. Gradually shift to using more questions and thereby guide the employees in specifying their own small steps.

CHECK PERFORMANCE

Visualize the coach standing on the sidelines, stopwatch in hand, checking the runner's speed. Checking is the manager's responsibility. Frequent checking allows quick action at the first sign of trouble, before a serious problem develops. And it makes the manager accessible for questions and guidance. Sometimes the Check step is called "management by walking around." Check at different times. Avoid making a rigid routine, such as dropping by every afternoon at 3:00 to count the output, which encourages people to look good at those times.

Use Performance Charts

USE CHARTS AND GRAPHS. They are welcome additions to any arena of competition. Posting performance graphs can motivate in a number of ways. High performers are obvious and others become aware of these superior performances. Average and poorer performers learn how they stand relative to others, making realistic goals easier to define. Posted charts increase peer acknowledgment, thus removing the burden from the supervisor of being the sole source of acknowledgment.

Posting the performance of individual players highlights individual contributions and stimulates intragroup competition. It's often used effectively with sales, for example. To solidify the team, on the other hand, it is more effective to post group performance charts, which are is a powerful motivator for stretching.

When employees chart their own performances over several days or weeks, patterns emerge and progress becomes evident. Research has indicated that when companies implement self-charting, performance of the variable charted improves dramatically. Self-charting also provides immediate feedback, which encourages self-acknowledgment for "on-TASC" performance and stimulates correction of drops of output.

ACKNOWLEDGE

MANY PEOPLE BELIEVE THAT MONEY is the most powerful reward for good work. Actually, the most potent, consistently available reinforcer is attention. Wanting to be acknowledged is universal. In fact, a strong argument could be

Attention is a powerful motivator. Use it! made that promotions, raises and perks are reinforcing because they are symbols of acknowledgment. We use them as concrete measures of our ability. Yet, it is easy for managers to get caught up in daily demands and become stingy in giving positive attention.

It is easy to get caught up in paying too much attention to the actions we don't want repeated instead of those we do.

Giving attention doesn't take long. In fact, whenever inter-acting with others, we constantly give and withhold atten-tion, usually without deliberate thought. For example, it is easy to give late employees the stink-eye while ignoring those who come in on time or to criticize poor performers while ignoring those whose meets our expectations. Coaches, on the other hand, realize that acknowledgment is a critical step in training and motivation.

Directly acknowledge on–TASC performance by com-menting on specific actions. Avoid vague superlatives, "Good Job!", which gives little feedback. Don't fall into a routine of mindlessly saying "Thank you." It is too easy to do this without giving genuine attention. Comments point-ing out specific actions are far more effective. "The report is thoroughly researched and well presented" is far more effective than "Good report, Thanks."

Tailor Your Attention

TAILOR ACKNOWL-EDGMENTS to the individual. Use the employees' metaphors, and speak in terms of their issues.

TASC+ Dos and Don'ts

DO	DON'T
Tell	
Describe what the person is doing.	Infer motives or feelings.
Be specific and concrete.	Be abstract and general.
Be objective.	Be judgmental.
Use performance indicators (quantitative indicators).	Use absolutes always/never.
Describe one standard or expectation at a time.	Describe more than one standard or expectation at a time.
Be concise.	Ramble, repeat, go off on tangents, Justify, defend, apologize.
State facts.	State rumors, suppositions, and generalizaitons.
Ask	
Use open-ended questions.	Ask leading questions or closed (yes/no) questions.
Seek facts.	Ask "why" questions.
Get all relevant information.	Be vague. Say only what is wrong. Tell employee.
Keep an open mind. Use active listening.	Jump to conclusions. Argue. Be inpatient or distracted. Use platitudes or generalities.
Ask for suggestions.	Tell or judge. Ignore suggestions.

Specify	
Be specific.	Be vague and ambiguous.
State what is wanted.	State what is not wanted.
Negotiate with employee.	Ignore employee input.
Check	
Vary when and how much.	Always say or do the same thing.
Use chart/graphs including self–charts, if feasible.	
Acknowledge performance.	Acknowledge before performance.
Acknowledge on-TASC performance	Acknowledge irrelevant performance.
Acknowledge publicly. Encourage.	
Tailor to the individual.	Use pat-phrases.

For example, if an employee is ambitious, a comment such as "That's the kind of idea that'll help you get ahead around here" can be highly reinforcing. To a more socially oriented employee, "You've done a lot to improve communications" would probably be more effective.

Acknowledge On-Tasc Performance

Focus on On–TASC performance by paying attention to ways in which the person is performing as desired. Pay attention to on–TASC actions, those that move toward a plan of action negotiated in the Specify step. Vary when, how often, and what actions you acknowledge. Anything that becomes routine tends to lose it motivational power. But even worse, when following a routine, we stop paying attention.

Acknowledge Publicly

HAVING WORK ACKNOWLEDGED in front of others (also in newsletters, on plaques and so forth), can be very rewarding to employees. Harness peer pressure and peer attention in the service of on-TASC performance. Encourage employees to acknowledge and reinforce each another. Peer acknowledgment removes the burden from you of always having to be there and helps encourage team spirit and a strong social support system.

Encourage Self-Acknowledgment

SELF-ACKNOWLEDGMENT IS THE CORNERSTONE of high self-esteem. It helps people get through attention dry spells. And knowing how to acknowledge oneself is essential for self-starting and self-directing. With TASC+, autonomous employees take the lead in setting their goals and in working out and implementing their action

FLEXIBLE COACHING TOOL

REMEMBER, YOU ARE A COACH and your job is to motivate your team to peak performance. To accomplish this you must teach them to be good team players by coaching them in the rules of the game and rewarding them for scoring and for throwing the ball to other players.

TASC+ is a tool managers can use to coach employees with dramatically different work styles. It provides a structured, yet flexible way to guide the work without making more autonomous employees feel encumbered. Simultaneously, TASC+ provides a process for keeping informed and for overseeing independently working employees. TASC+ takes maximum advantage of self-starting skills and employee creativity, while providing a way of eliciting participation while focusing on problem solving.

At the same time, TASC+ can be adjusted to employees who require more direction. TASC+ guides managers in being more active during Specify with employees lacking self-directive skills. By asking questions and breaking goals into action steps, TASC+ provides a way to help these employees develop problem-solving and self-directing skills. Begin by being directive during Specify, and over time guide employees in taking more active roles in shaping their project goals and accompanying small steps objectives.

Techniques employed by coaches and personal trainers, including those who coach canine athletes—show dogs—are taken from behavior modification methodology, which involves the use of rewards and feedback according to scientifically verified social-learning principles. The techniques are most apparent when watching dog trainers who give a treat, a pat, and a "good boy" when the pooch performs well. I'm not suggesting that employees are trained dogs! Rather that dogs and humans—as well as horses, rats, cats, raccoon, pigeons, chickens—have a lot in common when it comes to motivation. Pigeons can learn to peck at a grid that runs a machines. Rats can learn to run a maze. The learning principles are the same from humans all the way down to the lowliest creature. Of course, we humans are infinitely more complicated than dogs and horses.

Part Two

How Performance Is Established & Maintained

4

How Behavior is Acquired

UNDERSTANDING HOW BEHAVIOR IS LEARNED or "acquired" shows why punitive or disciplinary actions should be avoided or used with caution. Understanding basic principles of conditioning or learning is useful in determining the why's and how's of problematic behavior. You can use the principles to help employees unlearn problem behavior that interferes with their work, and to learn new more productive behaviors. Understanding learning principles is also useful in determining practice steps in training programs. Additionally, the principles can be useful in modifying your own behavior—which is essential if you are to keep up with the accelerated pace of change.

REFLEXIVE BEHAVIOR

REFLEXIVE BEHAVIOR IS LEARNED through a process called "classical conditioning", which was discovered by Pavlov in his experiments with dogs. The diagram on the next page illustrates how this form of learning works. At step one Pavlov presented meat—the *un*conditioned stimulus (UCS)—to a hungry dog, and the dog responded with the *un*conditioned response of salivation. It is called "unconditioned" because salivating is a reflexive or unlearned stimulus-response association. Salivating at the sight and smell of meat is hardwired into the dog's basic operating system and not programmed or conditioned.

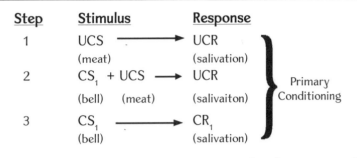

Step	Stimulus	Response	
1	UCS $\longrightarrow$	UCR	
	(meat)	(salivation)	
2	CS_1 + UCS $\longrightarrow$	UCR	Primary
	(bell) (meat)	(salivaiton)	Conditioning
3	CS_1 $\longrightarrow$	CR_1	
	(bell)	(salivation)	

Next, Pavlov rang a bell at the same time that he presented the meat to the dog. This is called "pairing" because the sound of the bell ringing was paired with the presentation of the meat. Again, the dog responded by salivating. Pavlov paired the ringing sound with the meat several times. Finally, he rang the bell but did *not* present the meat and the dog still salivated. The dog's operating system had learned to salivate at the sound of a bell. The bell is the conditioned or learned stimulus and the salivation is the learned or conditioned response (CS). The association is called "conditioned" because dogs don't normally salivate at the sound of a bell. The response is learned.

Phobias

PHOBIAS OR IRRATIONAL FEARS as well as emotional reactions to certain situations are acquired through classical conditioning. Typically the conditioning occurs during a traumatic event. Suppose, for example, that you were riding a horse and it threw you off. Responding with fear to being thrown through the air is hardwired into your biological operating system. Thus, flying through the air is the unconditioned stimulus and the fear you experienced is the unconditioned response.

In the course of this incident, your intense fear is paired with sitting on a horse so that your operating system would probably learn to respond fearfully to sitting on a horse—and possibly to the sight or even thought of a horse. Folk wisdom tells us that you should get right back on the horse, because by doing so you break the fearful association and thus unlearn or "extinguish" your fear of being on a horse.

Higher Order Learning

CONSIDER PAVLOV'S DOGS ONCE AGAIN. In step four, Pavlov paired a light with the bell and the dog salivated at the sound as before. After repeating this procedure a number of times, the dog salivated at the sight of the light alone. This is called higher-order conditioning, because a conditioned stimulus was used in the pairing.

Step	Stimulus	Response	
4	$CS_2 + CS_1$ (light) (bell)	CR_1 (salivaiton)	} Higher-Order Conditioning
5	CS_2 (light)	CR_2 (salivation)	

Most emotional reactions are learned through the process of higher-order conditioning. Suppose an employee has learned to respond anxiously to criticism. If this person feels criticized by you she may learn to respond anxiously to your presence, even when you are not being critical, because you were paired with the aversive stimulus of criticism. Through higher-order conditioning, you could become a conditioned stimulus that elicits anxiety.

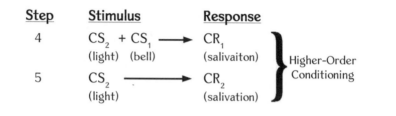

Higher-order conditioning is one way in which some people learn to display strong emotional reactions to certain minority groups or nationalities—even though they have had little or no personal contact with these groups. Higher-order conditioning also refers to the way in which words can have different connotations to different people.

VAGUE ANXIETY

A PERSON NEED NOT BE AWARE OF THE PROCESS, for conditioning to occur. Similarly, the selection of the conditioned stimulus is not a conscious choice in most cases. Anything that is *present in the situation* when a person experiences an aversive stimulus might become paired with that stimulus, and thus take on the power to elicit that same emotional response. For example, in the case of a critical boss, the office in which the critical remarks are made might also come to elicit anxiety in the person who was the object of criticism.

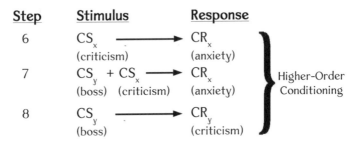

Step	Stimulus	Response	
6	CS_x (criticism)	CR_x (anxiety)	Higher-Order Conditioning
7	$CS_y + CS_x$ (boss) (criticism)	CR_x (anxiety)	
8	CS_y (boss)	CR_y (criticism)	

People who experience a lot of vague anxiety might be conditioned to respond with anxiety to many stimuli of which they are unaware. The color green, for example, might elicit anxiety in someone who, as a child, was severely spanked on a green carpet; small rooms might elicit anxiety because the spanking occurred in a small room. So that when in the presence of green or in a small room, this individual might feel vaguely anxious and be unaware that small rooms and the color green are eliciting this anxiety. Positive emotional responses to environmental stimuli are learned in the same manner.

In most cases conditioning extinguishes or dissapates and loses its hold on the individual because the unconditioned stimulus is never again paired with the conditioned stimulus. For example, in the case of the hungry dog, if the meat is never again paired with the bell, the dog will eventually stop salivating at the sound of the bell.

SELF-PERPETUATING

WHEN THE CONDITIONED RESPONSE IS ANXIETY or another strong emotion, however, the conditioning can become self-perpetuating because the sensation of anxiety is itself uncomfortable. Thus, when the conditioned response is anxiety, the feeling of anxiety is continually paired with the conditioned stimulus and is continually reconditioning the person. Thus, the person who was spanked on the green carpet might continue to respond with anxiety to the color green, even if such a punitive incident were never to occur again because the anxiety itself is distressful and cements the association.

Generalization

CONDITIONING IS NOT A STATIC PROCESS; it may generalize or become more discriminative. Conditioning "generalizes" when stimuli similar to the conditioned stimulus can elicit the conditioned response. The classic experiment that established this phenom- enon was the case of an eleven-month-old child, "Little Albert." By repeatedly pairing a loud noise (unconditioned stimulus—UCS) with a white rat in front of Albert, re- searchers were able to condition the child to cry—a fear response—at the sight of a white rat alone. The psy- chologists who performed the experiment discovered that after the conditioning Albert also cried at the sight of other white furry things, such as a white rabbit, a white dog, and a hairy Santa Claus mask. In this case, the condi- tioning "generalized" or spread to several white furry objects.

Discrimination

DISCRIMINATION IS ESSENTIALLY THE OPPOSITE PROCESS. Discrimination occurs when the conditioned stimulus elicits the condi- tioned response only under certain conditions. Discrimina- tive learning takes place when there is a third stimulus that is present *each time* the pairing occurs but that is not present when the pairing does not occur. For example, anxious employees may learn to discriminate among a critical boss's expressions. Suppose that the boss is critical only when he frowns; but when he doesn't frown, he does not criticize. In this case, an employee could learn to respond anxiously when the boss frowns but not otherwise.

VOLUNTARY BEHAVIOR

B. F. SKINNER DISCOVERED THE PRINCIPLES of "operant conditioning", which is also called instrumental learning, and is the process by which most behaviors of concern to managers are learned. Voluntary behaviors, such as making a sales pitch, key punching, and gossiping, are acquired through operant conditioning. Respondent behaviors, such as anxiety attacks, acquired through classical conditioning, as described above, are maintained through operant conditioning.

In operant conditioning the consequence—what happens immediately *after* the behavior—is crucial. Reinforcing consequences increase the likelihood that the behavior will recur and punishing consequences reduce that likelihood. For example, a pretentious engineer might throw a tantrum in the presence of certain environmental cues such as a request that he do his own word processing. The probability of his throwing tantrums in the future will be determined by the consequences of that behavior. If the supervi-

TYPES OF CONSEQUENCES

	Added	Removed
Something Positive	Positive Reinforcement	Extinction
Something Negative	Punishment	Negative Reinforcement

sor gives him special attention or finds someone else to do the typing—both rewarding consequences, then the tantrums will probably recur more frequently. If, on the other hand, the engineer is reprimanded or deprived of a privilege—both punitive consequences, then his tantrums will probably recur less frequently.

Reinforcement is a consequence that makes a behavior more likely. Notice that the definition is based upon effect and functionality. Positive reinforcement occurs when something positive is presented or "turned on" after a behavior. For example, the supervisor who commiserated with the tantrum-throwing engineer positively reinforced the engineer's tantrum behavior because commiseration, which is a kind of positive attention, followed the tantrum. If, on the other hand, the supervisor found someone else to do the engineer's word processing, the tantrum behavior would have been negatively reinforced because something negative was removed or "turned off" when the engineer did not have to do the word processing.

Punishment is a consequence that makes a behavior less likely. There are two types of punishment. Having something negative or unpleasant presented or turned on is experienced as punitive. By reprimanding to the engineer, the supervisor punished the tantrum behavior. Being reprimanded is a negative event after the tantrum behavior. Having something positive removed or withheld—turned off is also punitive. Depriving the engineer of a privilege would be punishment of the tantrum behavior because something positive is withheld.

Consequences

GENERALLY, BEHAVIORS THAT OCCUR OFTEN—be they desirable or undesirable—are "maintained" by positive consequences, and behaviors that occur infrequently are "suppressed" by negative consequences. Think of positive consequences as turning on something good—positive reinforcement, or turning off something bad—negative reinforcement. Think of negative consequences as turning off something good or turning on something bad, both of which are experienced as punishment.

TYPES OF CONSEQUENCES

Positive Consequences

Turning on something good (positive reinforcement)

Turning off something bad (negative reinforcement).

Negative Consequences

Turning off something good (extinction)

Turning on something bad (punishment)

Identifying Consequences

BECAUSE CONSEQUENCES HAVE SUCH A STRONG INFLUENCE on how often a behavior will occur in the future, identifying them is an important step in specifying the problem. The best way to identify a behavior-consequence pattern is through observation. Notice and write down what happens after the behavior occurs. Is there anything that seems to be turned on or off after it? Is there a pattern or recurring event? Is there more than one consequence? When Georgia observed what happened after Otto made a negative comment, she discovered a curious thing. Her own behavior was a consequence! She consistently responded with defensive comments to Otto's negative remarks. If we hypothesize that Otto enjoys Georgia's defensiveness (positive consequence), we can say Otto's negative behavior is maintained by the positive reinforcement of Georgia's defensive commenting.

Generally, behaviors that occur often—be they desirable or undesirable—are *maintained* by positive consequences, and behaviors that occur infrequently are *suppressed* by negative consequences.

Often there is more than one consequence. For example, Georgia found that Otto's negative comments were followed by positive attention like chuckling and knowing looks from the other salespeople. The attention from others is probably a more powerful reinforcer than is Georgia's defensiveness. Had she stopped observing as soon as she had identified one consequence, she might have failed in her change program.

REVIEW:

IN THE FOLLOWING SITUATIONS identify the behavior and its consequences.

Situation 1: A claims adjuster trainee handled five claims. Three claims had missing information, and two claims were complete. The supervisor commented on the thoroughness of the two completed claims.

ANALYSIS: Completing claims was reinforced by a positive comment. Not completing claims was being extinguished by the absence of a response. We would expect the trainee to be more careful in the future to complete all items on claims.

Situation 2: The previous supervisor of the word processing pool allowed those keypunchers who completed their assignments rapidly to take discretionary time. The new supervisor stopped the practice, and insisted that all keypunchers look productive at all times.

ANALYSIS: Rapid word processing was punished by the new supervisor. The supervisor has turned off something positive—discretionary time. We would expect typists to slow down and exhibit various negative emotions, such as irritability.

Situation 3: A new employee completed the first assignment promptly by the deadline, and handed it to the supervisor. The supervisor made no comment.

ANALYSIS: The employee's on-time behavior is being extinguished by the supervisor's lack of response. We would expect a decline in work completed on time. Additionally, the employee may be less enthusiastic about working.

Situation 4: William submitted a proposal to the planning committee that contained several cost-effective changes. In William's presence, his supervisor spoke to the department director and made positive comments about the proposal.

ANALYSIS: William's suggestions were reinforced. Commenting positively about William's work is a positive reinforcer. Making such positive comments to people in important positions in the company is especially powerful. We would expect William to submit more cost-saving proposals.

Situation 5: Bob spent several evenings and most of the weekend putting together an outline for a new sales promotion. His supervisor responded by pointing out three typos.

ANALYSIS: Bob's conscientious work was punished by ignoring his going to extra lengths to complete the out come and by criticizing minor details. We would expect that Bob would be less likely to work after hours and to be less motivated in general.

Situation 6: Alice completed the quarterly report a
day early and gave it to her supervisor. The
supervisor gave her an additional assignment to
complete during the extra time she created.

ANALYSIS: Alice's rapid work was punished, unless
Alice perceives extra assignments as positive, that
is, as an opportunity to get ahead. We would
expect that Alice would slow down in her work
and that her motivation would decline.

Chained Behavior

THUS FAR WE HAVE REVIEWED how a single behavioral event is learned,
but most work performance is comprised of a complicated series
of numerous behavioral events. The principle of chained behavior
explains how performance is prompted and maintained. The
figure on the next page depicts the dual consequence/antecedent
relationship of the behavioral events involved in such a simple
performance as making a sale.

Almost all work performance is a chain of behavioral events.

Functionally analyzing the ABCs that make up a performance chain is important in three ways. First, it is a guide
for the training director who wants to teach a particular
performance. By breaking the performance into its chain of
behavioral events, the trainer can arrange learning experiences to teach each behavior in the chain. Second, analyzing the chain assists managers in identifying the locus of
the problem when performance is inadequate or incomplete. That is, a manager can observe the discrete behaviors of an employee who is unable to carry out a performance successfully, so that the manager will know where
to intervene by having identified which behavioral event
needs to be learned or modified. Finally, by examining
chains, managers can identify behavioral events that are
irrelevant or counterproductive to desired performance.

MAKING A SALES CALL

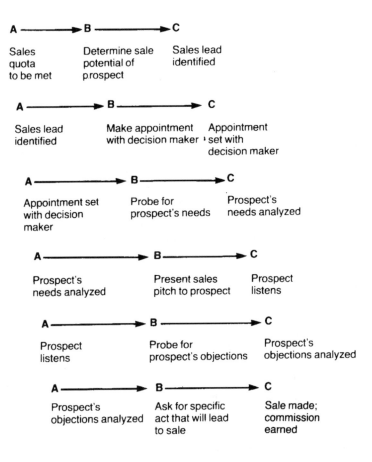

A ———————▶ B ———————▶ C

Sales   Determine sale   Sales lead
quota   potential of   identified
to be met   prospect

A ———————▶ B ———————▶ C

Sales lead   Make appointment   Appointment
identified   with decision maker ᴵ set with
                                   decision maker

A ———————▶ B ———————▶ C

Appointment set   Probe for   Prospect's
with decision   prospect's needs   needs analyzed
maker

A ———————▶ B ———————▶ C

Prospect's   Present sales   Prospect
needs analyzed   pitch to prospect listens

A ———————▶ B ———————▶ C

Prospect   Probe for   Prospect's
listens   prospect's objections objections analyzed

A ———————▶ B ———————▶ C

Prospect's   Ask for specific   Sale made;
objections analyzed act that will lead commission
                   to sale   earned

5

Vicarious Learning

N EMPLOYEE DOES NOT HAVE TO ACTUALLY ENGAGE in particular behavior to learn that it will meet with a particular consequence. We learn vicariously by watching other's behavior and observing the consequences they receive. This phenomenon is known as *modeling*. For example, if you observe your friend petting a neighborhood dog and then being bitten by it, you will probably avoid petting that dog even though you were not bitten by it. You learned vicariously through modeling that you may be bitten if you pet that dog.

Modeling is used extensively in all types of training. When learning to play tennis the instructor demonstrates the different kinds of swings while you observe what movements lead to hitting the ball over the net. A sales trainee can learn to give a sales pitch by watching the trainer giving a sales pitch. Trainees will learn more rapidly, if after watching a model, they then practice giving a sales pitch themselves and are reinforced for skillful portions.

A person does not necessarily even have to actually observe a behavior/consequence sequence to learn the probable consequences of that behavior. For example, your friend can tell you that she was bitten by the dog after petting it. Based on this information, you know that you're likely to be bitten if you pet the dog. This is a form of *symbolic learning*. Through the use of words—symbols—and abstract concepts you can learn contingency relationships. Being instructed or reading instructions is another form of symbolic learning.

SUPERSTITIOUS BEHAVIOR

SUPERSTITIOUS BEHAVIOR ATTEMPTS TO INFLUENCE a consequence when there is actually no causal relationship between that consequence and the superstitious actions. Blowing on dice before rolling them probably does not influence the roll just as knocking on wood probably has little influence over future events. The ace pilot who carries a talisman when flying is engaging in superstitious behavior. The person who pushes the elevator button several times is engaging in superstitious behavior, because pushing a button more than once does not bring the elevator any faster.

Superstitious behavior is established through chance. Suppose that the wiring in your car is defective so that you must turn the key several times in order to start the car. If you turn the key in vain, then bang on the dashboard and the car starts on the next key turn, you might mistakenly assume that banging on the dashboard resulted in the car's starting. In fact, the starting of the car after banging on the dash was a coincidence. Yet the car did start—consequence—after you banged on the dashboard—behavior. Essentially this is how superstitious behavior is established.

Superstitious behavior tends to be resistant to extinction because it is maintained by a variable schedule of reinforcement. Because there is no real cause-effect or contingency relationship, the desired consequence occurs occasionally by chance.

   Superstitious behaviors that are maintained by negative reinforcement are extremely resistant to extinction. Ace pilots carry charms so that they will not crash. Each time they fly while carrying the talisman and don't crash—a negative consequence that was withheld—their charm-carrying behavior is negatively reinforced. Only if a pilot were to crash several times while carrying the charm would that particular behavior be extinguished. The pilot being killed is a rather dramatic way to extinguish charm carrying!

SYMBOLIC PROCESSES

INDIVIDUAL BEHAVIOR PATTERNS are influenced by what we think about the situation—cognitive mediation. Thus, although rats may respond in a very predictable fashion to the presence of an antecedent cue and to the subsequent consequences, employee behavior is affected by their perception of the cues and by their anticipation of the consequences. Feelings, physical sensations, thoughts, fantasies, or visual images can function as antecedent cues, as behaviors, or as consequences in the same manner as overt actions do. For example, a sexual fantasy may function as an antecedent cue that elicits sexual behavior, as a positive reinforcer for the behavior of looking at attractive people, or as a behavior itself.

Individual behavior patterns are influenced by what we think about the situation.

Cognitive-symbolic processes play an important role in self-instruction and in self-reinforcement. One person may respond to a particular antecedent cue, such as an insult, by instructing herself to count to ten; another person may reinforce himself by thinking positive thoughts about himself. Self-reinforcement is an important component of self-esteem and it plays an instrumental role in maintaining what could be called self-directed behavior. The department self-starter probably uses a lot of self-instruction and self-reinforcement.

Cognitive-symbolic processes influence a person's perceptions of an antecedent cue. If you offer to take an employee, who is a vegetarian, out for a steak dinner, he or she may respond with hostility rather than with the expected appreciation. The employee may have used various thoughts and images to change the invitation from a positive to a negative event. Such internal processes can also influence our perceptions of consequences. You may intend to reinforce an employee by using praise, but if that person thinks, "I know he's just saying that to get me to write the report," then the reinforcing power of the praise is negated. Because of the existence of such cognitive-symbolic processes, modification of complex work behavior can be difficult.

6

How Cues Trigger Performance

ANTECEDENTS ARE EVENTS that *signal* that a certain behavior should be performed. They stimulate the behavior and are somethings called "stimuli". In some offices where employees goof off and gossip, antecedent cues, such as the supervisor leaving the room or talking on the phone, let them know when they can get away with it.

Antecedent cues can be established in two ways. With reflexive behaviors, like heart rate, flinching, sweating, the antecedent usually gains its power through association or pairing. Returning to Pavlov's dogs, when an unlearned stimulus, such as the smell of meat, is paired repeatedly with a neutral one, such as a bell, the neutral stimulus will eventually elicit salivation by itself—without the presentation of meat. In other words, the bell becomes a cue that signals the likelihood that meat will soon be forthcoming and thereby elicits the salivation. If this conditioned salivation is then reinforced repeatedly, the association between the bell and salivation becomes permanent and it will not be necessary to pair the bell with the meat to maintain the association.

Little Albert provides another example. He learned to cry at the sight of a white rat because he associated it with a loud and frightening noise. This learning generalized to white rabbits, white dogs, and a hairy Santa Claus mask. Now suppose Little Albert sees a rat or a Santa Claus—the antecedent cue or conditioned stimulus—and begins to cry—the learned or conditioned

response. Suppose when his mother hears him crying she gives him a lollipop. The mother's attention and tasting the lollipop are positive consequences. If this sequence were repeated a number of times, Albert would probably learn that the sight of a white rat or a Santa Claus is a cue to cry, which will bring a lollipop and Mom's cuddles. Thus, the power of the white rat—antecedent—to evoke crying—would have been established through classical conditioning and maintained with lollipops and Mom's attention—positive consequence—through operant conditioning. It would never again be necessary to pair the loud noise with the rat, because the crying behavior would be maintained by the reinforcement of his mother's attention and receiving a lollipop.

Antecedent cues are established by repeated association with a particular behavior-consequence sequence.

When a behavior is consistently reinforced or punished in the presence of a particular stimulus, that stimulus becomes an antecedent cue that signals the person to the likely consequences of that behavior in that situation. Again, notice the use of functionality and probability in the definition. Stated another way, antecedents signal a person to the "if-then" or contingent relationship between a particular behavior and its probable consequence—that is, if I do this now, then a particular event is likely to happen.

Stimulus Control

ANTECEDENTS CAN BECOME SO POWERFUL that they can evoke certain behavior. For example, because ashtrays are usually present when one smokes cigarettes, the sight of an ashtray alone can evoke smoking. Each time the smoker enjoys smoking after seeing an ashtray, the association is established even more firmly. Expressed in terms of the ABCs, the ashtray is the antecedent cue, smoking is the behavior, and enjoyment is the reinforcing consequence. In short, behavior is influenced by what comes before it and by what follows it. Antecedents "elicit" or "set the occasion" for the behavior to occur, and the consequences "strengthen" or "weaken" the behavior response.

Stimulus control develops when certain behaviors occur in the presence of some antecedents and not in the presence of others.

Suppose that whenever Jeff tells John a juicy story, John responds with interest, whereas whenever Jeff gossips to Susan, she responds with irritation. John's interest reinforces the gossiping, and Susan's irritation punishes the gossiping. Very quickly Jeff's gossiping behavior will come under stimulus control so that John's presence becomes an antecedent stimulus that signals that gossiping is okay in John's office, while Susan's presence becomes an antecedent that discourages gossiping.

Stimulus control is established through discriminative learning in which the individual learns that a particular behavior pattern, such as wearing sexy clothes, will be reinforced in the certain situations, such as when with friends at a party, but punished in other situations, such when attending a church service.

It is through stimulus control or discriminative learning that an employee can learn such things as where and when to look busy, who can be trusted with privileged information, how to identify a defective product, who will provide an answer to a difficult problem, or when he can get away with stealing office supplies.

Response Generalization

A PARTICULAR RESPONSE CAN GENERALIZE to more than one situation or cue. Generalization occurs when a particular behavior is reinforced or punished in the presence of a variety of cues. Generalization can also occur when a behavior is reinforced in the presence of a cue similar to but different from the original one. This is the way in which many children learn to respect people who wear uniforms, for example. A child might be praised for acting respectfully toward a police officer, and because a police officer's uniform is very similar to a security guard's uniform, the child might then act respectfully toward security guards. After many such experiences, the child learns to act respectfully toward anyone wearing a uniform. Over time, acting respectfully might generalize from people in uniform to anyone in a position of authority.

The phenomenon of generalization is important in any training program. It would be a waste of time to train people to deliver a sales pitch if they could do so only in the presence of the trainer. The trainer is hoping that what the trainees learn during the training will generalize from the classroom to the work setting. Unfortunately, in all too many cases it doesn't, so that the benefits of training are questionable.

7

Principles of Reinforcement

FOR A STIMULUS TO FUNCTION as a reinforcer, it must meet two conditions. It must be experienced as positive by the recipient employee and applied contingently.

IF-THEN

To FUNCTION AS A REINFORCEMENT the action must be *contingent* on the performance of a specific behavior. That is, the delivery of the reinforcement must be based on an "if-then" relationship. *If* the behavior is carried out, *then* the specific consequence will follow. A behavior change strategy usually includes alteration of if-then relationships. The manager who wants to modify gossiping must change the contingent relationship from "if Jeff gossips, then I will listen" to "if Jeff gossips, then I will look away and if Jeff talks about work-related topics, then I will listen." In this example the manager has "rearranged the contingencies."

DESIRABLE

To BE EFFECTIVE, the reinforcement must be desired or experienced as positive by the person being reinforced. Whereas a lollipop might be an effective reinforcer for Little Albert, it will not be an effective reinforcer for the pompous engineer. Although some consequences—such as praise and other positive attention—are desired by most people, it is a mistake to assume that one reinforcer will be desired by all employees. What constitutes a desired consequence varies considerably from individual to individual, which means that identifying and utilizing a desired consequence is an essential step in developing a successful behavior change strategy.

TIMING

THE POWER OF A REINFORCER to establish and maintain a behavior is determined by when and how often it is delivered. The timing of reinforcement refers to how long after the target behavior occurs that the reinforcement is delivered. The sooner the reinforcement is delivered, the more effective it will be. Common sense tells us that to say "thank you" for a favor immediately has more impact than to say "thank you" a month later.

When and how often you respond to employees has tremendous power.

Obviously, in a work situation it is not always possible to deliver a reinforcement immediately after the performance of each desired behavior. As a general principle, to establish or teach a behavior, the reinforcement should be delivered *each time* the behavior is carried out, but once the behavior is learned it can be maintained most efficiently by intermittent reinforcement. There are five different schedules of reinforcement, with each one having a different effect on the target behavior.

Sooner the reinforcement the more effective.

Continuous Reinforcement

A SCHEDULE OF CONTINUOUS REINFORCEMENT is one in which a positive consequence follows *each* enactment of the target behavior. If you nodded approvingly every morning when your assistant arrived on time you would be continuously reinforcing your assistance is promptness in arriving to work. Continuous reinforcement results in a steady high rate of responding as long as the reinforcement continues to follow every response. This schedule is most appropriate for establishing or teaching new behaviors and for increasing the frequency of existing behaviors.

Continuous reinforcement has two drawbacks: First, the behavior weakens or undergoes extinction rapidly when the reinforcement is discontinued. For example, assistants who are accustomed to being thanked each time they get coffee for their supervisors are likely to stop getting coffee if they are not thanked a few times.

The second drawback is that the reinforcer may lose its desirability to the person and thereby its power to reinforce. If a manager uses the word "terrific" in response to every suggestion an employee makes, "terrific" may lose its power to reinforce suggestion giving.

To maintain a behavior once it has been established, the schedule of reinforcement should be gradually changed from continuous to intermittent.

Intermittent Reinforcement

When reinforcement follows some but not all occurrences of the behavior, it is said to be intermittent. There are two kinds of intermittent reinforcement: the ratio schedule and the interval schedule. Ratio schedules refer to reinforcements received after a particular *number* of responses, whereas reinforcement available only after a *lapse of time* is on an interval schedule.

Both ratio and interval schedules may be either fixed or variable. A fixed schedule is one in which a *specific* length of time or number of responses is required before the reinforcement is delivered. Piece work is an example of a fixed-ratio schedule. The 40-hour workweek is an example of a fixed-interval schedule. With piecework the worker is paid for completing a specific number of items; with the workweek the worker is paid for spending a specific amount of time on the job. With both

Unpredictable reinforcement promotes continuous responding.

the fixed-interval and the fixed-ratio schedules, every response is not reinforced and the reinforcement is delivered intermittently and *predictably*.

RATE OF RESPONDING

FIXED SCHEDULES HAVE ONE MAJOR DRAWBACK: The rate of responding usually drops immediately after the reinforcement is delivered. This is because the responses that occur immediately after the reinforcement are *never* reinforced. Therefore, in a fixed schedule we find that the frequency of responding is highest just before reinforcement and lowest just after reinforcement. The longer the fixed time or the larger the fixed number of responses required, the longer will be the pause after reinforcement before responding is resumed.

In a fixed schedule the frequency of responding is highest just before reinforcement and lowest just after reinforcement.

For example, in theory a paycheck is supposed to reinforce work, whereas it is actually contingent on the length of time—number of days and/or hours—one spends on the job. Thus, we would expect that the rate of absences among salaried workers would be highest at the beginning of a pay period—the day after receiving a paycheck—and lowest at the end of the pay period—the day the paychecks are issued. Likewise, those working on a task or piecework basis are likely to work harder when the task is near completion. This explains why many pieceworkers find it difficult to begin a new project. The pieceworker who must complete many items before being paid is likely to pause longer at the beginning than a worker who must complete fewer items before being paid. Similarly, we would expect more absences at the beginning of a monthly pay period than at the beginning of a weekly pay period.

The paycheck is supposed to reinforce work, but it is actually amount of time one spends at the job site that is being reinforced.

Variable Schedule

A VARIABLE REINFORCEMENT SCHEDULE is one in which the length of time or the number of responses required to obtain the reinforcement varies randomly. Because receipt of reinforcement is unpredictable, variable schedules do not usually result in workers' pausing immediately after reinforcement. The reason for this is that, owing to the *unpredictability* of the variable schedule, the first response after receiving a reinforcement might also be reinforced, whereas there is always a fixed space between reinforcements with the fixed schedule. That is, in the fixed schedule the first response after reinforcement would never be reinforced. Consequently, that first response would be subject to extinction which results in a short pause, whereas when the reinforcement is unpredictable, the first response may be rewarded.

If, for example, paychecks were issued on a variable-interval schedule, we would predict that the rate of absenteeism at the beginning of the pay period would drop, since the workers would not know on which day they would be paid. Likewise, casino slot machine players are likely to continue playing at a high rate after getting a win because sometimes they will win twice in a row and sometimes they will win only after many turns—variable ratio schedule. Making sales is another example of a variable ratio schedule.

The salesperson never knows how many calls will be required to secure a sale, which may explain the dogged perseverance of many salespeople.

There is an exception to the general principle of continued high rates of response when using variable schedules. When the average interval or ratio required to secure reinforcement is very big, the person may pause after the reinforcement. That is, although sometimes the first response or first time segment is reinforced, the probability of this decreases as the interval or ratio increases. Hence, the person learns that another reinforcement will usually not be forthcoming for a long time or until many responses have been evidenced. A quality control inspector in a company that produces very few defective items is more likely to become lax immediately after finding a defective item than is an inspector who works for a company that produces many defective items. In general, when the average intervals or ratios are moderate, response will remain constant and high. Thus, behavior is most efficiently maintained by variable or random schedules of reinforcement.

RESISTANCE TO EXTINCTION

A BEHAVIOR IS SAID TO BE RESISTANT TO EXTINCTION when it continues after reinforcement is discontinued. The spurned lover who continues to call and ask for second chances is an example. Behavior that has been maintained on an intermittent schedule is more resistant to extinction than is behavior that has been maintained on a schedule of continuous reinforcement. Suppose that the call button for the elevator in your building is defective and you discovered you must push it three times to call the elevator. You are likely to continue to use that button to call the elevator as long as it always comes after three pushes.

However, if one day you push the button three times and it doesn't come, you may continue to push it three, six, or even nine times more. But if the elevator still does not come, you will probably give up and use the escalator instead. If for a few days in a row the elevator does not come after pushing the button three or six times, you are likely to stop approaching the elevator altogether and go directly to the stairs each day.

On the other hand, the manager who is trying to stop the engineer's temper tantrums may occasionally give in to the engineer, without realizing that giving in intermittently makes the tantrums extremely resistant to extinction. By contrast, if the manager has always given in and then abruptly stops doing so, the tantrums will probably be extinguished rapidly, unless they continue to be reinforced by other workers' attention.

THE PREMACK PRINCIPLE

RECALL THAT REINFORCEMENT IS FUNCTIONALLY DEFINED as a consequence that makes the performance of a certain behavior more likely. Many people mistakenly assume that reinforcement is synonymous with reward. That is not the case. A reward is probably a reinforcement, but a reinforcement is not necessarily a reward. For example, the quality control inspector's behavior is probably reinforced by identifying a defective item, although one can hardly consider spotting a defective item to be a "reward".

The Premack Principle of reinforcement states that a high-probability behavior—a behavior that occurs frequently-can reinforce a low-probability behavior—a behavior that occurs infrequently.

This principle is important for managers, because when utilized contingently it can help managers use work to reinforce work.

Suppose that a salesperson calls on a lot of old clients, but has very few new clients. The number of new clients called upon can be increased if calling on old clients is made contingent on calling upon a specified number of new clients. Basically, it is a matter of doing the least liked work first and the most liked work second. Generally, any behavior that is not painful or unpleasant for an employee and that the employee enacts frequently can be *used* as a reinforcer. For example, if a secretary uses the copy machine several times a day (high probability behavior), then going to the copy machine can be used to reinforce a low-probability behavior such as filing.

In order to be effective as a reinforcer, going to the copy machine must be contingent on doing a specified amount of filing. For example, *if* the secretary files 20 folders, *then* the secretary can go to the photocopy room. Common high-probability behaviors include looking at one's watch, reading email, drinking coffee, smoking cigarettes, and talking on the telephone. Good self-managers often bribe themselves into performing tasks they don't like by using the principle. We call this "self-discipline."

Reinforce Work
With Work

THE INCENTIVE PROGRAMS USED to reduce tardiness and absentee-ism illustrate the effectiveness of one of the simplest intervention strategies—the addition of a reinforcer. The feasibility of this strategy for first-line managers con-cerned with individual employee behavior problems is limited: Most managers do not have discretionary funds from which to draw incentives, and there are potential problems in placing one or two employees in a division or office on an incentive system.

Rearrangement of existing contingen-cies is a simple reinforcement strategy that bypasses these problems. Here, there is no addition; rather, the se-quence of events is rear-ranged so that an existing reinforcer follows the behav-ior to be increased.

Opportunity to do favored work is an often overlooked powerful reinforcer. Tasks that employees tend to do first can be used to reinforce those they tend to leave until last. Salespeople, for example, often call their old clients first while putting off calling new clients. This can be reinforcing because old clients are usually easier to sell to and getting sales is reinforcing. Consequently, it is often difficult for the sales manager to motivate salespeople to call on new clients.

Researchers demonstrated how to use the Premack Principle to solve this problem. Two part-time telephone solicitors were employed to sell new appliance service contracts (warranties) and to renew old ones. During the first sessions the salesmen could phone warranty and renewal customers in any order they chose. As expected the percentage of calls which resulted in sales was higher for the old contracts (31 and 27 percent, respectively) than it was for new contracts (13 and 10 percent, respectively). In other words, renewing previously existing contracts that were about to expire was a high -probability behavior, whereas selling new contracts to new customers was a low-probability behavior.

During the next ten sessions the salesmen's opportunity to make five renewal calls was made contingent on their selling a new contract, not just calling a new customer. Each salesman was instructed that after he made one warranty sale he could make five renewal calls, which usually resulted in a sale. Rearranging the contingencies in this manner had a significant impact on the percentage of warranty sales made. Both salesmen increased the number of warranty sales (10 and 21 percent, respectively). Unexpectedly the researchers discovered that both salesmen made more renewal sales as well (4 and 22 percent, respectively).

During the final ten sessions the men were told that they could once again call customers in any order they chose. The percentage of new warranty sales took a dramatic nose dive. After the contingencies for warranty sales were removed, neither salesman made any new warranty calls. The number of renewal sales also dropped. For the first salesman, the percentage dropped only one percent, whereas the percentage of renewal calls by the second salesman dropped by 21 percent.

Although there are few systematic evaluations of the application of the Premack principle in organizational settings, this study points to its potential cost-effectiveness. Not only did the low-probability behavior of making new warranty calls increase substantially, but the high probability behavior of making renewal sales increased as well. In other words, productivity increased in both cases, and there was no of the expense involved in giving bonuses.

The intervention had more of an impact on one of the salesmen: The second salesman's performance increased more than did the first one's. Stated another way, the reinforcer was more effective with the second salesman, which points to the importance of tailoring the reinforcers to the individual.

An interesting feature of this study is that the researchers did not tell the salesmen how sales should be accomplished, only that they must be closed before the salesmen could call the renewal customers Although one salesman showed a greater increase than the other, both showed a significant increase compared with their previous performance. Leaving it up to the individual salesmen to determine their own method of improving their efficiency not only resulted in increased sales, but the salesmen reported that they felt they were being allowed to follow their own unique styles rather than being encouraged to imitate that of someone else. The company was perceived as finally recognizing their individual talents, and the salesmen actually enjoyed producing a higher sales rate. This contrasts with the commonly reported feeling of being made by the company to run faster to keep up. The salesmen reported that their success genuinely reflected their own talents. On the other hand, the salesmen's program did not employ the use of goal-setting. Goal-setting has a powerful positive impact on performance. Had the salesmen been assigned goals, their-percentage of warranty sales may have increased even more.

8

Escape, Avoidance & Punishment

THE PRINCIPLES of aversive antecedent cues and negative reinforcement explain how many nonproductive work behaviors are established and maintained. Often an employee engages in various work behaviors not to gain a positive consequence but to *avoid* or *escape* a negative one. To illustrate how avoidance and escape behaviors are established, consider the case of Joe. Suppose that Joe has been criticized several times by his boss for loafing. And suppose that Joe has learned that when he does work appropriately that his boss does not criticize him. This is a situation in which the presence of the boss—an aversive antecedent—stimulates work behavior—avoidance behavior—which is negatively reinforced by the *absence* of criticism—something unpleasant doesn't happen.

However, when the boss is not present, Joe is likely to loaf because such behavior in the boss's absence does not bring criticism. In fact, loafing in the absence of the boss might be positively reinforced by the pleasure of surfing the net or by socializing with others, as examples. Thus, Joe's loafing is under stimulus control. When the boss is present, Joe avoids criticism by working but when the boss is absent, Joe loafs and enjoys the pleasure of socializing and surfing. The boss and the company have a problem: Working to avoid criticism or other negative consequences is inefficient. The only way the boss can increase Joe's efficiency is to monitor Joe's work continually—often called micro-management—with the implicit threat of criticism if work is not performed. Doing this would likely ignite a vicious cycle of monitoring and avoidance.

ESCAPE

Escape behavior is similar to avoidance in that it is established and maintained through negative reinforcement, which involves the withholding or removal of something unpleasant. But whereas avoidance implies that the person engages in a behavior within the situation, escape behavior means that the person leaves the situation entirely. Absenteeism, for example, is frequently an escape behavior.

Suppose that during the biweekly supervisory meeting, Ruth is frequently criticized. The day of the meeting could then become an antecedent cue that signals the likelihood of getting criticized. If Ruth is absent on the day of the meeting, she escapes the possibility of criticism, so Ruth's absenteeism is negatively reinforced. If this is the case, Ruth's absences on the day of the meeting are likely to increase.

Threats

Threat of discipline and other punitive measures can have far-reaching negative consequences for the company and the manager as well as for employees. Managers who use punitive methods inadvertently teach employees to be unproductive workers. Such employees become limited in their capacity to function appropriately in a work setting and in their ability to gain positive consequences such as feelings of accomplishment, self-esteem, promotions, pay increases, and so forth. Use of punitive control methods is one cause of the disgruntled, uncommitted, and unproductive workforce that is found so often today.

If the person is successful in avoiding or escaping the negative consequence, then the behavior doesn't occur for you to observe.

Avoidance and escape dynamics can make performing a functional analysis especially difficult. Instead you must guess what is likely to happen if the person failed to avoid it. This is why identifying the antecedents in a functional analysis is important. Preceding cues can provide clues as to what is controlling the avoidance.

PROBLEMS WITH PUNISHMENT

Most psychologists advise against the use of punitive methods, and advocate positive methods of behavior control. For one thing, punishment usually results in only a *short-term* behavior change and it is often accompanied by undesirable and unpredictable side effects. As illustrated in the case of Joe and the critical boss, mangers who use punishment can themselves become a cue signaling the likelihood of punishment. Not only does this usually result in many avoidance and escape behaviors such as absenteeism, nonproductive work, and obsessive agreement with the supervisor; but it can become almost impossible for the manager to function as an administrator of positive reinforcement.

It becomes physically impossible for you to deliver positive reinforcement to someone who is avoiding you.

A punitive boss who attempts to be positive, tends to arouse the suspicions of subordinates, who discredit any positive reinforcement delivered as some kind of manipulation.

• Unpredictable Emotions

DYNAMICS OF EMOTIONAL RESPONSES are complex and not completely understood, making it difficult to predict how an employee will respond to a punitive experience. Punitive experiences commonly elicit dysfunctional emotional responses such as angry outbursts, breaking of equipment, threats, and sabotage.

• Temporary Suppression

RELATED TO AVOIDANCE AND ESCAPE BEHAVIOR is the problem of a temporary suppression of the undesired behavior. The undesired behavior, such as Joe's loafing, is suppressed only as long as the punitive boss is present; but as soon as the boss leaves, the undesired behavior usually returns.

• Inflexibility

IT IS NOT UNCOMMON FOR A BEHAVIOR to be viewed as undesirable at one time, but in another time and place to be considered highly desirable. Yet, as a result of past punishment, the behavior may be inhibited or permanently suppressed. For example, the suggestions of a management trainee may be suppressed by derogatory remarks from the supervisor, so that later on, when the supervisor actively solicits suggestions, the trainee may be unwilling or unable to generate any ideas.

• Punishment Begets Punishment

A SERIOUS PROBLEM WITH THE USE OF PUNISHMENT is that punishment begets punishment. The more people use punishment, the more likely they will be to use it again. Punishment is inherently reinforcing to the manager inflicting it. The punishing act is usually followed by the immediate cessation of the undesired behavior, which is negatively reinforcing to the manager. There tend to be a number of accompanying positive reinforces as well, such as feeling potent, the employee cowering and possibly doing what the manager wants. In short, the consequences of punishment tend to reinforce the manager for being punitive.

The punishing act is usually followed by the immediate cessation of the undesired behavior, which is negatively reinforcing to the manager.

Once again we have a vicious cycle, one that results in an increase in the frequency of punishment. Suppose a foreman's job is threatened by a drop in production—an antecedent trigger. So the foreman upbraids the subordinates and threatens that heads will roll if there isn't an immediate increase in productivity—punishing behavior. Subordinates respond by working faster and production increases—reinforcing consequence. But it is short lived. After a few days the subordinates slow down again. When they do the foreman is likely to again engage in punishing behavior because it has been both positively and negatively reinforced in the past. That is, the foreman's threats were positively reinforced by the increase in production and negatively reinforced by the temporary relief from worrying about termination.

• Does Not Teach Any Skill

THE FINAL PROBLEM WITH THE USE OF PUNISHMENT is that, although it suppresses undesirable behaviors, it does not teach desired behaviors. An awkward teenager asking for a date may be

punished by being rejected by the prom queen. The rejec-
tion will tend to suppress asking for a date, but it does not
teach the teenager social graces so that he can extend an
invitation that will be accepted.

EXTINCTION

EXTINCTION IS THE PROCESS BY WHICH CONDITIONING or learning is
reversed or unlearned. In general, conditioned or learned
responses established through Pavlovian conditioning can
be extinguished by continued presentation of the conditioned stimulus in the absence of the unconditioned stimulus. Thus, if the conditioned and unconditioned stimuli are
never again paired, the conditioned stimulus will lose its
power to elicit the conditioned response. For example, if
the dog in Pavlov's experiment had heard the bell ring
numerous times yet did not get any meat, the bell would
eventually loose its power to make the dog salivate.

Exceptions

THERE ARE TWO EXCEPTIONS TO THIS GENERAL RULE. First, if the
conditioned response is itself aversive, the conditioning will
tend to remain intact. Responses such as anxiety and fear
are inherently unpleasant. Consequently, these uncomfortable sensations themselves become associated with the
conditioned stimulus, such as the white rat causing Little
Albert to cry, and tend to maintain the learned response of
crying.

The second exception is the case in which the conditioned response is followed by reinforcement. Each time
Little Albert cried, his mother gave him a lollipop. The
lollipop is a positive consequence that reinforced and
maintained crying. In this situation we would not expect
the crying in response to a white rat to extinguish even
though the rat is never again paired with a loud noise. We'd
predict that Little Albert would have a life-long neurosis
and spend hours with a shrink trying to understand his
numerous seemingly irrational anxieties.

Avoidance and escape behaviors are difficult to extinguish because they are negatively reinforced. For example, a dog who has learned to jump out of a compartment in response to a flashing light and an electric shock will probably continue to do so

Escaping is negatively reinforced by the very act of escaping.

when the light flashes even though the light is never again paired with the shock. Jumping out of the box is negatively reinforced because the dog avoided the shock—even when none would have actually occurred. Escape behavior is negatively reinforced by the very act of escaping.

In contrast, behaviors established through Skinnarian conditioning can be extinguished by withholding the controlling consequence. For example, when gossiping is ignored and no longer followed by attentive listening, which is a reinforcing consequence, it will probably stop. The process of extinction can be functionally similar to negative punishment. Negative punishment is the withholding or removal of something positive. When the gossip, who is accustomed to receiving attentive listening, is ignored that lack of attention can be experienced as punishment.

Reward incompatible behavior to avoid the unpredictable aspects of negative reinforcement, it is best to simultaneously positively reinforce a behavior that is *incompatible* with the behavior being extinguished. For instance, talking about work-related topics is incompatible with gossiping, because one cannot do both at once. To extinguish gossip behavior most efficiently, a manager should ignore all gossip talk and listen attentively to work-related talk. This principle of reinforcing a desired incompatible behavior rather than punishing an undesired behavior can be applied to all areas of the work environment. Examples of incompatible behaviors include standing-sitting, tension-relaxation, loafing-working, laughing-crying, frowning-smiling, and assertiveness-passivity.

The principle of reinforcing a desired incompatible behavior rather than punishing an undesired behavior can be applied to all areas of the work environment.

Part Three

Strategies to Get Peak Performance

9

Behavior Mod

BEHAVIOR MODIFICATION, which makes up the foundation of the coaching approach to management, is an empirically-based method of changing performance. Changing the frequency of the target behavior is a common denominator of all behavior mod intervention strategies. The goal is to stop problem behaviors and to increase productive ones.

STEPS OF BEHAVIOR CHANGE PROGRAM

1. Identify the target behavior.
2. Measure current levels of performance.
3. Intervene.
4. Evaluate.
5. Maintain.

IDENTIFY THE TARGET BEHAVIOR

THE FIRST STEP IN A BEHAVIOR CHANGE PROGRAM is to determine the "target behavior" to be modified. The *target behavior* may be an undesirable behavior to be reduced or eliminated, or it might be a desirable behavior to be increased. Behaviors undesirable in a workplace setting include tardiness, procrastination, and goofing off, as examples. Promptness, task accomplishment, and attentiveness are examples of desirable workplace behaviors. You will discover as we move through this material that what constitutes "behavior" is broadly, yet, precisely defined.

You may be surprised to know that the definition of behavior goes beyond visually observable actions. Internal or "covert behavior", such as thinking and visualizing, operates by the same principles as external or overt behavior, such as typing accuracy and making suggestions, and can be modified by use of the same principles. Cognitive psychologists describe thinking as "self-talk". Self-talk is the stream of consciousness going on all the time in our minds. We are talking to ourselves! Self-talk is an internal or covert behavior that operates by the same scientifically verified principles as those that we will be discussing in this book.

While we can only observe the actual overt actions of others, we make guesses about their internal behaviors by observing how they act and listening to what they say. With ourselves, on the other hand, we don't have to guess, we can directly observe our own internal behaviors. Employees can observe their internal behaviors. As a coach, you can assist employees in changing certain unproductive attitudes (which is a kind of self-talk) and poor work habits, much as a personal trainer might guide someone struggling to stick to their daily exercise regime. For example, the trainer may assist the struggling exerciser in identifying and changing his self-defeating thoughts (a bad attitude) towards his ability to pump iron to a more beneficial way of thinking about it. Similarly, a salesperson might avoid calling a particular client on the phone because of the anxiety she experiences when talking with him. As a coach, you may guide the sales person in changing his anxiety-provoking self-talk. While employees with "bad attitudes" can be problematic, generally, however, most of your coaching effort will probably target observable workplace behavior.

Focus on the
Desirable Behavior

IT IS EASY TO GET CAUGHT UP in viewing problems as certain negative behaviors that must be stopped—i.e., reduced in frequency, which inevitably leads to punitive techniques. Punishment suppresses the behavior that is punished, which is why it is used.

However, punishment can backfire by triggering unpredictable emotions, which can become associated with you, the manager, so that your very presence—or even thinking of you—can become anxiety- or anger-provoking. Obviously, it's pretty difficult to do an effective job of running your shop if your employees get upset by your presence. Yet, it is natural to reach for a punitive approach. We all do it. Reacting to employee problems with punishment is almost a knee-jerk response. But the gains are short-term while the dangers can be far-reaching.

Another problem with punishment, which was mentioned earlier but needs repeating, is that punishment suppresses the behavior punished but does not teach the person what to do instead. Worse, when the instead is left to chance the undesirable behavior can be replaced with another problem behavior. So punishment is something of a crapshoot—you leave a lot to chance. Reinforcement, on the other hand, enhances and encourages the behavior reinforced. Using reinforcement is much less risky.

Positive behavior change interventions are more reliable, but it can take much longer to see results. With punishment you get an immediate result—which is very reinforcing to you, the punisher, launching a vicious cycle of punishment quickly followed by short-term cessation of the problem, followed by return of the problem or new problems, which triggers more punishment.

The skilled managerial coach holds back from immediately responding to employee problems to take time to analyze the factors at play in order to identify the actions that she wants the employee to perform. One technique

for accomplishing this is to notice your tendency to respond punitively as a signal to remind yourself that you are
focusing on what you want to suppress and then to *purposefully* instruct yourself to identify what it is that the
employee should be do instead—the desired behavior.

REFRAME THE PROBLEM

IDENTIFYING A POSITIVE BEHAVIOR to enhance is not always so easy,
especially since we tend to be blinded by viewing the
situation as a problem behavior to be stopped. When the
problem behavior is undesirable, translating it into desirable behavior de-emphasizes punishment and focuses on
positive behavior change techniques.

To break out of the negative focus, ask yourself: *What
do I want the employee to do instead?"* By making this
simple change in the way of looking at the problem and
you will become significantly more motivating to your
employees. We notice what we focus on. When you focus
on the problem to be reduced, you will notice incidences of
the problem to which you'll tend to respond negatively.
When you focus on the desires performance to be increased, you'll notice incidences of improvement and the
simple act of your noticing it tends to be reinforcing.

The way that you view the world is learned and becomes a habitual viewpoint. You see the glass as half
empty or as half full. You see imperfections, problems,
mistakes, or you see improve-
ments, challenges,
progress. If you want
to be a masterful
coach and people
handler you
must train
yourself to
focus on the
desired perfor-
mance to be
increased.

Involve the Target Person

A NUMBER OF ETHICAL CONCERNS present themselves when you set out to systematically alter another person's behavior, especially if that person is an underling. We tend to view this as being Machiavellian, which has all kinds of negative connotations. On the other hand, we manipulate one another with every response we make. We can not not manipulate because we are a part of the ABC's of other people's lives. Rather than fall mindlessly into punitive responses, for example, why not respond mindfully, so that you consciously endeavor to enhance the behaviors you seek instead. Fortunately, the ethical dilemma can be largely resolved by using the TASC+ Coaching Model to involve the employee in each step of the change program. When employees actively participate, the change process speeds up and chances of successful change vastly increases. An additional benefit is that the employee learns valuable *self*-management skills and evolves into an ever more skilled employee.

The underlying premise of scientifically based behavior management is that behavior—including undesirable or anti-productive workplace behavior—is promoted by events in the environment rather than by internal needs or neurosis of some sort. Behavior change is accomplished by arranging environmental conditions to promote unlearning undesirable behavior and relearning desirable behavior. Change strategies are empirical, which means that they are rooted in scientific research, and systematic, following five basic steps

ESTABLISH A BASELINE

IT IS IMPORTANT TO ESTABLISH A BASELINE, which tells how often the problem behavior occurs, before making any intervention efforts. Knowing the current frequency of performance provides a marker by which to measure improvement and to determine if your change efforts are working.

Baseline is established by counting how often the behavior in question occurs. Sometimes you will focus on the frequency of the problem behavior which you want to reduce; other times you will count the frequency of the desired behavior that you want to increase. Sometimes you will count both frequencies.

INTERVENE

THE FIRST STEP OF INTERVENTION is to analyze the behavior dynamic to determine what is keeping it going. This involves identifying the ABCs—the Antecedents, Behaviors and Consequences. When you understand this dynamic, you will have a good idea of specific actions you can take to break the cycle and change the behavior in question.

Assess Current Skill Level

WHEN YOU HAVE IDENTIFIED THE DESIRED BEHAVIOR—what you want the employee to do instead of what she is currently do-ing—then you must ascertain if the person has the capabil-ity to do what is desired. Assessing the person's skill or inability is important in determining how to intervene in the problem behavior cycle. If the employee knows how to perform the desired behavior but is not doing so, then you need to enhance (increase the frequency) a dormant behavior. This would call for implementing a reward program or a contingency management strategy. If the person does not have the skill necessary to perform, then a shaping technique that teaches the employee how to perform the desired behavior is needed.

> When the employee has the skill but is not performing use *contingency management*.
>
> When the employee does have the skill use a *shaping technique* to teach how to perform.

MAINTAIN

IF YOU SIMPLY STOP YOUR INTERVENTION EFFORTS when the employee shapes up and is performing as desired, the employee is likely to slip back into the old behavior patterns—especially when factors in the situation have not changed. Suppose, for example that through your coaching an employee who spent a lot of time gossiping, works at his desk with focused attention when you give him positive attention for doing so. If you stop giving positive attention, the likelihood is virtually 100% that he will slide back into gossiping, rather than working. This is especially true when coworkers encourage gossiping.

So it is vital that you plan in advance for when the employee has gotten up to speed and is performing as desired. You need to determine a method for maintaining the behavior. Sometimes this will involve establishing certain cues to prompt a continuation of the desired behavior. Other times, it may involve rearranging the environment to remove cues, such as relocating a co-worker, who initiates gossiping, to a different area. In most cases, you will use contingent reinforcement, which may include teaching the employee to pat himself on the back.

EVALUATE

WE TEND TO THINK OF EVALUATION as something that comes at the end that tells us how well our program did. In behavioral coaching evaluation is an ongoing process. Just as a track coach times each sprint, so too ongoing measurement is useful in determining progress. In fact, the evaluation itself is a change tool. When the athlete gets the feedback from her last sprint, she has a marker to surpass in the next effort.

10

Pinpoint

IN OUR DAILY LIVES WE USE NUMEROUS ABSTRACT WORDS—such as immature, hostile, capable, feminine, independent, motivated—to describe other people's behavior. Such words work fine in casual conversations but they do not work well in a behavior change program because these words have too many meanings. Returning to Otto's case. Georgia said, "Otto is a salesman with a lot of experience. The problem is that he is continually challenging my authority." This sounds pretty bad, but do we really know what Otto's is doing? What is meant by "challenging my authority"? What does Otto actually *do?* Is it Otto's facial expression or something he says? Or does Otto go over Georgia's head with requests and complaints? "Challenging my authority" doesn't tell us.

Vague descriptions must be translated into words that stand for specific behaviors.

The first task is to specify or "pinpoint" the target behavior. This requires that abstract and vague descriptions, such as challenging my authority, be translated into words that stand for definitive behaviors. In general, you can get to the definitive level by asking, "Is there a distinct beginning and end to the behavior? Can it be counted?" Accountability—count-ability—is an essential component of a change program. Coaches on the track field carry a stop watch to measure time. Personal trainers count minutes on the treadmill.

Another way to zero in on the specific level to ask, "What must the person do in order for me to say that the annoying behavior has occurred?" And finally, "Can it be reliably observed—including with self-observation? Can it be heard, or seen, or felt, or smelled?" When you can answer all of these questions affirmatively in terms of specific occurrences, then you will have identified a "behavioral event."

Counter

When Georgia asked these questions of Otto's behavior, she identified that he makes negative, uncooperative, disapproving, defeatist comments about her program. Such comments can be counted and independent observers can agree on the whether or not a particular statement is a negative comment about Georgia's program.

Specify the Situation

GEORGIA'S TASK IS NOT YET COMPLETE. To complete the description of the problem it is necessary to think of the behavior in combination with the situation in which it occurs — *behavior-in-situation.* Georgia needs to specify the situation in which the behavior that challenges to her authority actually occurs. When does Otto make negative comments about Georgia's program? Let's look at an improved description of the problem with Otto: "During the weekly staff meeting, Otto who is an experienced salesman on my staff, frequently makes negative—uncooperative, disapproving, defeatist—comments about my program."

Is "making negative comments about program" a behavior? Let's ask the questions: Can the comments be counted? Yes, we can determine if a comment is positive or negative and a comment has a beginning and an end. What must Otto do before we can say that a negative comment about the program has occurred? He must make a statement that is negative comment, connoting disapproval, predicting failure, or advocating noncooperation. In a controlled laboratory experiment, the operational definition of negative comments about a program would be far more precise, and only specified kinds of statements would be permitted to count. However, as a practicing manager you don't need to go to that length, but you do need to be able to determine whether or not each of Otto's comments about the program is negative, neutral or positive.

The answer to the final question is helpful here: Can a negative comment about the program be reliably observed? Yes, two or more people listening to Otto could probably agree if a particular comment about the program is negative. We can now say that the problem behavior has been specified—Otto's negative comments about the program in the weekly staff meeting.

Here we have:

> **Behavior**: Making negative comments about
> program
>
> in
>
> **Situation**: Staff meetings

Is It Performance Related?

AFTER YOU HAVE IDENTIFIED THE BEHAVIOR-IN-SITUATION, you are confronted with the question: Is this behavior performance-related? Behaviors targeted for modification should be related to the employee's own performance outcomes or to the performance of other employees to such an extent that it influences accomplishment of company objectives. If the behavior has no impact on the accomplishment of organizational objectives, then using company time to change it would be inefficient and wasteful. If Otto's sales performance under the new program is exceptional and his negative comments do not appear to influence the sales performance of others, then Otto's negative commenting is probably not performance-related.

On the other hand, if Georgia responds to Otto's negative comments with "self-doubts"—silent self-depreciating self-talk—and these self-doubts result in her making defensive remarks to Otto, then Otto's behavior is performance-related in that it has an adverse effect on Georgia's performance. Under these circumstances it would be an appropriate target behavior to consider for a behavior change program. Alternatively, Georgia might consider a self-change program in which she alters her self-doubting self-talk and defensive replies to Otto's negative commenting in the staff meeting.

Collect Examples

IDENTIFYING THE TARGET BEHAVIOR is not always as easy and as obvious as it is in the case of Otto. Suppose a manager says, "Meredith is too aggressive." You already know this description is inadequate because it tells you nothing of the circumstances in which Meredith is aggressive or even what is meant by "aggressive." Suppose that in trying to clarify these points the manager says, "I don't know what situations she's aggressive in—she's always aggressive!" The way to break through this barrier is to observe Meredith and identify several instances of her aggressiveness. For example, the manager might observe, "Today, when another secretary asked Meredith to copy a flier she said 'No!' loudly and stomped out the door." And the next day Meredith was observed replying sharply, "Get it yourself!" when a file clerk asked her to pick up an extra cup of coffee at the canteen.

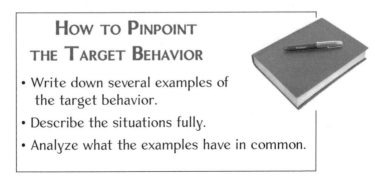

HOW TO PINPOINT THE TARGET BEHAVIOR

- Write down several examples of the target behavior.
- Describe the situations fully.
- Analyze what the examples have in common.

By observing and collecting specific examples, you can quickly identify specific behaviors in specific situations. Write down several examples of the target behavior. Describe fully the situations and analyze what they have in common. For example, looking for the commonality in the examples of Meredith's aggressiveness, the manager might write, "When asked to do a favor, Meredith tends to refuse in an ungracious manner". When the behavior occurs in several situations, it may be that the situations have something in common, such as "when Meredith is asked to do a favor". If you cannot identify a common thread, you probably have several different problem behaviors.

When the Desired Behavior
Is Not Occurring

OFTEN THE PROBLEM is something the person is *not* doing. For example, a manager might say, "Jack doesn't approach and greet customers." Jack *is doing* something else when the manager wants him to approach and greet customers. A complete description of the problem specifies the situation and what desirable behavior is not occurring as well as what undesirable behavior is occurring instead.

Jack's supervisor should specify the situation in which he wants the behavior to occur—when a customer enters the store—and then observe what happens instead of the desired behavior. For example, "Jack was talking with the inventory clerk (situation) when a customer entered the store. Jack ignored the customer as he continued to talk with the clerk." Such a description is much more useful than "Jack doesn't approach and greet customers". By including in the problem description what Jack is doing instead of greeting customers, you already have a good idea of where to aim your intervention. Instead of criticizing Jack for not greeting, it will probably be more productive to curtail socializing on the floor, for example.

Observe what happens instead of the desired behavior.

When The Outcome Is Inadequate

ANOTHER PROBLEM DIFFICULT TO IDENTIFY is an absent or inadequate outcome, such as uncompleted reports or unfilled sales quota. An outcome is not a behavior, but it is dependent on the performance of a chain of behaviors. Therefore, problem identification requires you to pinpoint the chain of behaviors necessary to produce the desired outcome. The location of the problem is the point in the chain at which the employee is not performing the behavior necessary to move to the next link. When you know the chain of behaviors necessary to produce the desired outcome, problem identification is simplified: You observe the person moving step-by-step through the task until you identify the breakdown.

IDENTIFY CHAIN OF BEHAVIOR

IN PROFESSIONAL AND TECHNICAL FIELDS managers often supervise people whose work is outside their own expertise. In these situations you can identify the chain of behaviors by asking the subordinate, observing a model, or seeking expert advice.

•Ask the Subordinate

IT IS A GOOD IDEA TO BEGIN WITH THE ASSUMPTION that employees know what steps are necessary to complete their assigned tasks and that they are aware of the obstacles they are experiencing. After all, they were employed because they had the requisite skills and experience. Subordinates may feel hesitant, but by asking questions you can help them talk about their difficulties.

Employees know what is holding them back. *Ask.*

This sets the stage for enlisting their cooperation in correcting the outcome problem. More importantly, it is a good opportunity for you to help your subordinates assume responsibility for their own work behavior. Rather than trying to change the behavior of the subordinates, you can use this as an opportunity to teach them to change their own behavior.

Consider Charles, the program director of a small town radio station. His problem is simple—he procrastinates. It takes him twice as long as necessary to finish the schedule of upcoming programs, which creates problems for all the other departments. Sales can't sell programs, because they don't know what's going on the air or when. Completing a schedule or a report is not a behavior; it is an outcome of a chain of behaviors. Thus, to say that Charles procrastinates does not focus on the problem behavior that results in delayed schedules.

During the coaching session, the station manager asked Charles about each step necessary for completing the program. Charles said, "I don't put off scheduling. It's that I have trouble with Rosemary. I need to get a projection of the topics of her editorials, but I have so much trouble dealing with her that I send memos. She doesn't respond right away and causes a delay." Further investigation revealed that Charles found it difficult to give Rosemary a directive, because she would question him. Consequently, he sent directives in memo form instead. Thus, the behavior-in-situation turned out to be not Charles's procrastination but giving Rosemary a directive (behavior) when she asked questions (situation).

•Observe a Model

WHEN THE EMPLOYEE CANNOT IDENTIFY THE BREAKDOWN in the chain of behaviors and you do not have sufficient expertise to identify the behavior links necessary to produce the outcome, then you can observe a model performing the sequence of behaviors. Football coaches, for example, spend a lot of time with the team reviewing video replays in slow motion to identify key moves that lead to successful plays. Identify other employees whose performance leads to successful outcomes and observe their step-by-step behaviors. Next, observe the employee while experiencing the difficulty and look for a breakdown in the behavior chain..

Football coaches replays in slow motion to identify key moves that lead to successful plays.

For example, if a couple of your salespeople are not reaching their quotas, you might observe your top performers' sales presentations. Then you could observe the less skilled salespeople in action while looking for the behaviors present in the stars' performance but absent in the less successful presentations. The discrepancy would illuminate the missing links in the behavior chain and point to the behaviors that they needed to learn.

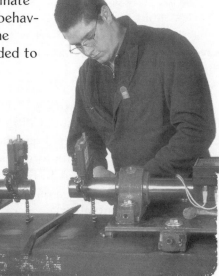

•Seek Expert Advice

WHEN IT ISN'T POSSIBLE TO ACTUALLY OBSERVE A MODEL, consult an expert. In this case, the expert is one who knows how to perform each behavior necessary for a successful outcome. After the expert delineates the necessary chain of behaviors, observe the employee's behavior, looking for the broken link.

Returning to the sales example, you might ask a consultant who has expertise in selling to describe the critical selling steps and the order in which they should be performed. You would then observe and compare the below quota salespeople's presentations to the sales expert's description.

11

Establish Baseline

O NE WAY in which scientifically based behavior change strategies differ from other approaches to managing people is the establishment of a baseline. Having a baseline provides a starting point, a marker, which provides a means of accountability and evaluation. It tells how often the problem behavior is occurring now—*before intervention.* The baseline allows for objective assessment of progress. When there is little or no difference between the baseline and the current level of performing, you can rapidly determine that your efforts are ineffective and that you should try something different. Gathering baseline information is cost-effective, and an essential step in a successful behavior change program.

Conducting the functional analysis and gathering baseline data frequently overlap, because both require careful observation. However, the type of observation differs. Antecedents and consequences are identified by recording *descriptions of events.* A baseline is established by *counting how many times the behavior occurs* and recording that number.

The most common difficulty encountered in gathering baseline data is being able to decide whether or not the behavior has occurred. This can be avoided by pinpointing the target behavior precisely enough so that you can determine if a particular instance is an occurrence of the target behavior—yes or no. Yes, Melody is talking on the phone; or no, she is not talking on the phone. Yes, Otto made a negative comment about the program; or no, he didn't.

If your description is vague or ambiguous, you will find out quickly because gathering baseline data involves counting each occurrence of the behavior-in-situation, which is hard to do when you're not sure what the behavior is or when it occurs. For example, Georgia's problem with Otto was that he was constantly challenging her authority. Georgia soon found that counting incidences of Otto's challenges to her authority was a lot harder than she had guessed it would be. The reason was that Georgia could not always determine which of Otto's statements were challenging and which were not. Georgia needed to refine her description of the target behavior. When Georgia specified the target behavior as "negative comment in the staff meeting about the innovative program" it was much easier to determine when a statement was or wasn't negative statement about the program.

Suppose Otto says, "I think we should reconsider each step of this program in light of the new developments in the market." Is this to be counted as a negative comment or not? Any answer besides a definite "yes" or "no" indicates that the target behavior has not been sufficiently defined. Georgia would reduce the effectiveness of her team and would limit Otto as well if she employed a change program that discouraged Otto's problem-solving comments. Before Georgia can continue collecting baseline data, she needs to return to the first step of specifying the problem behavior. When she can define "a negative comment about the program" clearly enough that she can classify any statement Otto makes as an incidence of the target behavior or not—then Georgia is ready to resume collecting the baseline data.

WHAT TO COUNT

SOMETIMES THE CONCERN IS how often the problem behavior occurs but the duration of its occurrences. Suppose the problem with Melody's personal calls was not that she makes call but that she generally talks for more than 15 minutes. To obtain a baseline, her supervisor would record the length of the calls.

As a rule of thumb, a baseline is obtained by counting the number of separate times the behavior occurs—*frequency*—or by counting the length of the occurrences—*duration*—or by counting the intensity of the occurrence—*degree*.

Sometimes the information needed to get a baseline has already been collected. Sources of behavioral data include payroll records to obtain absentee data, time cards for tardiness, and log records for speed of response, such as in police calls. Whenever possible, utilize such records—it saves time.

Behavior Occurrences

SOME NATURAL QUESTIONS ARE, "How do I count? What tool do I use?" There are a number of counting methods, the most obvious and traditional of which is the tally. The method is simple and we've all used it at one time or other. Each time you observe the target behavior, make a check on a piece of paper or on a 3" X 5" index card. At the end of the day or of the meeting, count up the checks and transfer this data onto your graph. Georgia counted Otto's negative statements during the staff meeting by putting hatch marks the corner of her agenda notes. At the end of the meeting, she recorded the number of negative comments on a graph. In this way she could determine the frequency of Otto's negative comments over time.

Counters

A SECOND TOOL YOU CAN TRY is a golfer's counter. The best is the type you wear on your wrist—it looks like a watch. These are particularly effective because you can use them without interrupting your activity or diverting your attention. Whether you prefer the tally or a physical counter, the point is to count. The method you use doesn't matter as long as you get accurate data, so devise a method that is easy and that works for you.

Self-Recording

THE BEST APPROACH is to have employees count and record their own behavior. For example, chronically late employees can record their time of arrival each day, packers on an assembly line can count the number of boxes correctly packed, a secretary can record the length of each personal phone call.

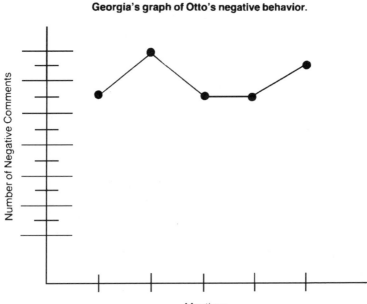

Georgia's graph of Otto's negative behavior.

Self-recording gives employees immediate feedback on their behavior. Interestingly when people count their own problem behaviors, they tend to change in the desired direction. That is, if it is a problem of excess, such as talking too long on the phone, or of insufficiency, such as completing too few items, behavior tends to decrease or increase depending upon which is desired, without any other intervention—just counting.

Intuitively, we all know the power of counting. Coaches and personal trainers use the simple but powerful tool of counting throughout their regime. When employees keep track of performance that they want to improve their performance and without undue effort. This simple tool is a secret of self-management and achievement. Make sure that you reinforce employees for collecting data on their own behavior.

There is no set length of time for collecting baseline data. You need to keep counting until you can see a consistent trend. If the target behavior occurs several times a day, then most likely a 3 to 4 day-long baseline would suffice. When there is a lot of variation from day to day, a longer baseline period will be needed. This counting should continue until you feel you understand the pattern of the target behavior.

GATHER A SAMPLE

IF THE TARGET BEHAVIOR OCCURS REGULARLY, the actual time involved gathering baseline data can be shortened considerably by using a time sample. A time sample is similar to an opinion poll. Just as those conducting the poll cannot interview everyone in the country, you probably cannot count every occurrence of the behavior. Opinion polls solve the problem by selecting a sample of people and interviewing them. With a time sample, you select a few short periods each day and count how often the behavior **Respond** occurs during the sample. For example, **to each** Georgia might select two five-minute time periods in each meeting to count Otto's **person** comments. **as an**

How the sample is selected is impor- **individual.** tant. If an opinion poll were to base its conclusions solely on the opinions of Californians, the results probably would not represent the country as a whole. So the pollsters use various method to randomly select people to interview from the entire country. The time sample, too, must represent the whole time period covered. Georgia randomly select the time periods by assigning a number to each five-minute period in the meeting, putting them into the proverbial hat, and select- ing two at random to use as her sample.

NOT A CRISIS TECHNIQUE

Behavior coaching techniques are foundation-building tech- niques—not crisis intervention—that require careful analysis before implementation. Scientifically based behavior change is an approach in which you become an applied behavioral scientist solving a problem. Each behavior change program is a unique challenge, because no two people are alike. What one employee finds reinforcing, another does not. What provokes one employee has no impact on another. To be an effective behavior coach, you need to understand and respond to each person as an individual. In part, you can accomplish this by observing, analyzing, and counting. By understanding each employee's uniqueness you can develop a change program suited to his or her individual needs.

You become an applied behavioral scientist solving a problem.

During coaching employees actively participate in modify- ing their own work-related behavior. You solve the problem at hand at the same time that you teach employees how to work and how to solve their work problems. Over the long run you are relieved from close monitoring and crisis intervention and have more time to invest in functions such as deciding, planning, coordinating, and directing.

Counting the target behavior continues during the intervention and is compared with the baseline to give an immediate indication of the effectiveness of the change program. Such data can be used as concrete evidence of your effectiveness as a manager. When the data moves in the desired direction—if the frequency of undesired behaviors decreases and that of desired behaviors increases—your intervention is working. If the trend plateaus or reverses, you know that it is time for troubleshooting. When the frequency of the target behavior reaches a predetermined goal, it is a signal to implement techniques that will maintain the behavior at that frequency—in other words, it signals that the intervention phase is complete.

12

Identify
the ABCs

*T*HERE'S A TENDENCY to want to intervene
immediately when we become aware of a
problem. It is difficult to withhold instituting a change because we want to do something about it
right now. However, careful observation of the problem
behavior is an essential step in a successful change program. Coaches always gather data on an athlete's current
level of performing as a first step in training, which they
use to determine where to intervene to improve performance and as a baseline for evaluating improvement.
Similarly, after identifying the target behavior, you must
analyze how that behavior is controlled and then establish
a baseline from which to measure the success of the
intervention. These three tasks can often be performed
simultaneously, but for clarity of discussion they are
presented here as discrete steps.

The ABCs—*Antecedents, Behaviors, Consequences*—is a way of thinking about behavior and its causes.

Behavior occurs within a context of what occurs before it—
the antecedents—and after it—the consequences. Viewing
problems in terms of the antecedents and consequences

that control it keeps us focused on events, rather than speculating about attitudes, willpower, morals and other ethereal factors. An event, however, is not labeled as an antecedent, behavior, or consequence because of something inherent in the event itself. Rather, it is the *function* that the event serves that determines its classification.

Consider the following sequence:

> Boss criticizes Joan. Joan starts crying. Ted sympathizes with Joan. Joan stops crying. Ted buys Joan coffee.

Can you identify which event is the antecedent? The behavior? The consequence? Your analysis—called a *functional analysis*—depends on which action is the focal point and what functions the other events serve relative to it.

The diagram shows a functional analysis of this series of events. As you can see, an event can *function* as an antecedent, a behavior, or as a consequence. For example, Ted's sympathy with Joan functions as a positive consequence and also as an antecedent to Joan's cessation of her crying. And, of course, Ted's sympathy is a behavior evoked by the antecedent cue of Joan's crying, and is negatively reinforced by the cessation of Joan's crying.

FUNCTIONAL ANALYSIS OF A VICIOUS CYCLE

A ⟶ B ⟶ C

| Boss criticizes Joan | Joan cries | Ted sympathizes with Joan |

A ⟶ B ⟶ C

| Joan cries | Ted sympathizes with Joan | Joan stops crying |

A ⟶ B ⟶ C

| Ted sympathizes with Joan | Joan stops crying | Ted buys Joan a cup of coffee |

What we see here is a "vicious cycle." Ted's sympathetic attention maintains Joan's crying behavior and Joan's
cessation of her crying maintains Ted's sympathetic behavior. However, experientially Joan and Ted each feel that the
other is "making" them behave the way they do, and neither is aware of how they stimulate and maintain the
other's behavior. This dynamic is particularly evident in
conflicts in which both parties point to the other as the
instigator of the problem. Most people are unaware of how
their actions and reactions control others, but are very
aware of how others' actions and reactions control them.

On the basis of this functional analysis, we would
predict that Joan will cry more when criticized by the boss
and Ted will sympathize more when Joan cries. A careful
functional analysis is an essential step in modifying a
problem behavior such as crying at work. The analysis
reveals the factors that prompt and maintain each behavior
in a cycle, which a manager can use to determine the most
appropriate intervention point.

ANTECEDENTS

ANTECEDENTS ARE EVENTS THAT OCCUR BEFORE BEHAVIORS that cue or
signal us as to which behaviors are appropriate in a given
situation. For example, the ringing of a bell at 8:00 A.M. is a
cue that lets assemblers know that work is about to begin.
An antecedent that is always present when a person
behaves in a certain way can actually develop the power to
evoke that very behavior, or at least set the occasion for it
to occur. For example, an advertisement for a delicious
steak dinner may evoke desire for such a steak—even in the
absence of physiological hunger; rock music may evoke
dancing; seeing an ashtray may evoke smoking; and so
forth. Usually we are un-
aware of the cues that elicit
our behavior unless our
attention is specifically
directed toward them.

**Antecedents signal
which behaviors
are appropriate in
a given situation.**

BEHAVIORS

BEHAVIOR IS DIVIDED INTO TWO BROAD CATEGORIES: reflexive and voluntary behavior. This is an important distinction, because there is a difference in the underlying processes by which these behaviors are learned.

Reflexive Behaviors

REFLEXIVE BEHAVIORS—sometimes called respondent behaviors—are not learned; they are present at birth, or develop as a result of physical maturing. These behaviors are hard-wired into the basic operating system and a person ordinarily has no control over engaging in them. They include physical reflexes such as the constriction of the pupil when a bright light is directed into the eye, the jerking of the knee when a doctor taps it in a specific way, or the startle reaction to an unexpected loud noise.

Reflexes are hard-wired into the basic operating system.

Although reflexive behaviors themselves are not learned, a person can learn to perform the reflex in the presence of something—a cue or "antecedent stimulus"—that ordinarily would not elicit that behavior. For example, to respond with fear to a loud noise is inborn, but through a process called "classical conditioning" a person can learn to respond fearfully in situations that are not physically dangerous. So while reflexes themselves are unlearned, a person can learn to carry them out in a wide variety of situations.

Voluntary Behaviors

VOLUNTARY BEHAVIORS—sometimes called instrumental or operant behaviors—are learned and not hard-wired into the person's basic operating system. Voluntary behaviors include such things as hitting a baseball, programming a computer, dancing, and typing. The process by which we learn voluntary behaviors is called "operant conditioning". Most behaviors of concern to managers are voluntary behaviors.

CONSEQUENCES

CONSEQUENCES ARE EVENTS that immediately follow a behavior. The kind of consequence—positive, negative, or neutral— exerts a powerful influence on whether a person will engage in that behavior again.

People are more likely to repeat a behavior that is followed by a positive consequence and less likely to repeat a behavior that is followed by a negative consequence.

For example, when the factory bell rings at 8:00 A.M., assemblers receive positive consequences if they begin working and negative consequences if they continue to socialize. We all intuitively understand the power of consequences, sometimes called rewards and punishments. As we shall see, consequences can be subtle and complicated.

13

Identify Reinforcers

*I*NCENTIVE PROGRAMS, BONUSES, FRINGE BENEFITS, and promotions are traditional contingency addition strategies. All too often, however, incentive programs prove costly and ineffective because they are not obtained contingently or because the incentives are not powerful reinforcers.

CONTINGENT

To BE EFFECTIVE in increasing and maintaining behaviors, the reinforcer must be desired by the employee and getting it must be contingent on the performance of a particular behavior. A dental plan given to all employees, for example, is rarely effective in motivating behavior change because it is not contingent. The power of a bonus is often lessened because the employee receives the bonus so long after the performance of the behavior, often many months, so that it is virtually ineffective as a reinforcer. Furthermore, benefits and bonuses may not be a high priority for the employee in question. Just because a benefit or bonus is not refused does not mean that it is actively desired.

DESIRED

OFTEN MANAGERS BELIEVE that they know what is, reinforcing to employees. Researchers asked managers and employees to rate the importance of ten factors in motivating employ-

Tailor your coaching strategies to individuals.

ees. Their answers revealed that managers had a very different idea about employee motivators than employees did. For example, employees rated "appreciation or deserved praise" as first, "feeling 'in' on things" second, and "understanding personal problems" as third in importance. In contrast, managers considered these factors to be the least effective motivators (eighth, tenth, and ninth, respectively). Managers rated as very potent motivators "good wages" (first), "promotion" (third), and "good working conditions" (fourth). Employee rated these factors as considerably less important (fifth, seventh, a ninth, respectively).

A survey conducted on its readership by *Psychology Today* underscored the degree to which managers misunderstand employees. Of 18 job factors explored, readers rated the following as the six most important: (1) chances to do something that makes you feel good about yourself; (2) chances to accomplish something worthwhile; (3) chances to learn new things; (4) opportunities to develop your skills and abilities; (5) the amount of freedom you have in your job; (6) chances you have to do things you do best. By contrast, those factors that have been traditionally assumed to be potent motivators fell low on the list. For example, job security rated eleventh, amount of pay rated twelfth, fringe benefits rated sixteenth, chances for promotion rated seventeenth, and physical surroundings rated eighteenth. Clearly, managers have a very different idea of what is reinforcing to employees than what actually is reinforcing. Money and fringe benefits are not the powerful motivators they have been assumed to be, and therein lies the problem. Managers too frequently assume that they know what is reinforcing. No wonder so many finely conceived incentive programs have failed! The solution to this dilemma is to observe employees as individuals and to ask questions.

The key is to discover what is reinforcing to the employee and then to insert it into the if-then statement.

The primary difference between the strategies of rearranging contingencies and of adding contingencies is that in the first, *current* reinforcers are used whereas in the second *more* reinforcers are employed. While contingency addition involves increasing reinforcement it doesn't require additional expense; rather it involves additional attention, additional opportunities for recognition and skill development, and additional privileges—usually more of those privileges that already exist.

IDENTIFYING REINFORCERS

POTENTIAL REINFORCERS ARE IDENTIFIED in the same way as existing reinforcers, but the emphasis is on asking employees about their experience. Employees are keenly aware of what they want and what they find rewarding. For one employee, it may be more or longer breaks; for another, it may be more involvement in decisions; for yet another employee, it may be the opportunity to work on tasks that will eventually lead to greater skills. Interviews with top-level executives has revealed that more autonomy, opportunities to build an effective team, and chances to feel like a winner are potent motivators. Most of the powerful potential reinforcers are readily available to managers.

Observation

OBSERVATION IS THE PRIMARY TOOL for discovering existing reinforcers. The necessity of detailed and systematic observation cannot be overemphasized. Pay particular attention to the consequences following behaviors that the target person performs often—high-probability behaviors—and activities or behaviors that the person chooses to engage in during discretionary time.

The technical definition of a reinforcer is "an event that increases the future probability of the behavior it follows." Therefore, those behaviors the target person performs frequently are probably followed by a reinforcer. It gets a little tricky when the reinforcer is avoidance of punishment. Such negative reinforcement is difficult to observe because we can't see what doesn't happen. Generally, it is not suggested that supervisors employ negative reinforcement in rearranging contingencies. That is, an if-then statement such as "If Betty makes a suggestion, then I *will not* criticize her" is less desirable than "If Betty makes a suggestion, then I *will* make an appreciative comment."

The use of negative reinforcers, which involves *withholding of punishment*, promotes working to avoid punishment and generally requires constant close monitoring of the employee. This obviously reduces the time supervisors have available for other management functions and tends to deprive employees of satisfaction in their work.

Look For What Follows Frequent Behaviors

THE SECRET IS TO IDENTIFY POSITIVE REINFORCERS that *currently exist* in the target person's environment and then to insert them into the if-then statement. The best approach is to identify several behaviors the person performs often, then look for what positive consequences follow those behaviors. Keep a record of each behavior and its consequences.

For example, Ralph's supervisor identified two of Ralph's high frequency behaviors: telling jokes and talking to the secretary. The supervisor noted that Ralph's joking behavior was usually followed by statements from the secretary indicating that she thought Ralph was funny and clever. Ralph's talking to the secretary was usually followed by her putting his work before that of other employees. This suggests that hearing that he is funny and clever and having his word processing projects completed first are reinforcing consequences for Ralph.

Betty's supervisor identified making agreeing statements and volunteering to do busywork as high-probability or frequent behaviors. For Betty the consequence of agreement was usually a statement attesting to her competence. Volunteering to do busywork was followed by comments indicating her indispensability. Betty's supervisor can consider these sorts of statements as possible reinforcers for Betty. Now Ralph and Betty's supervisors have some possible consequences to insert into the if-then contingency statement: "If Ralph is on time, then I will tell the secretary to make his work a high priority." "If Betty makes a useful suggestion, then I will comment on her competency."

SPECIAL ATTENTION REINFORCERS

Praise

Praise in front of others

Special work assignments

Reserved parking space

Choice of office

Selection of own office furnishings

Invitation to higher-level meetings

Choice of work attire

Social contacts with others

Solicitation of opinions and ideas

Choice Of work partner

Flexible job duties

PERSONAL TIME REINFORCERS

Time off for work-related activities
Time off for personal business
Extra break time
Extra meal time
Choice of working hours or days off

MONETARY REINFORCERS

Promotion
Paid days off
Company stock
Company car
Pay for sick days not taken
Pay for overtime accumulated
Tickets to special events
Free raffle or lottery tickets
Extra furnishing for office
Gift certificates
Dinner for family at nice restaurant
Personalized license plate
Personalized gifts
Special workstation
Business cards
Expense account

POWER REINFORCERS

Voice in policy decisions
Help set standards
Be a representative at meetings
More responsibility
Opportunity to learn new skill
Involvement in important decisions

Notice that there is an emphasis on "potential" reinforcers. The list are potentials, but not necessarily reinforcing to all employees. Employees are individuals. To be effective behavior coaching strategies must be tailored to individuals. A manager is a "handler" much like a coach may handle an athlete. Coach work with athletes to facilitate their performing at their peak, which is achieved by understanding each employee, as an individual—to learn what is rewarding to this unique person?

The more that the motivators you employ are tailored to the individual employees, the more power they have to influence their performance.

Observe what moves the employee; then arrange the contingencies to use the power of the motivator. This is done by inserting appropriate reinforcers into the if-then statement. For example, suppose being considered creative is reinforcing to Betty. And suppose that Betty's manager wanted to increase Betty's participation in the work group. Betty's manager could use Betty's desire to be seen as creative to motivate her to participate more. When Betty makes a suggestion, the manager might make a comment about its creativity to his own supervisor in Betty's presence.

Special attention used contingently can be a powerful tool for facilitating employees to perform at their peak. The radio station manager might take Charles out to lunch after he negotiated with Rosemary about getting the projection on time, as another example.

Use Frequent Behaviors

THE SECOND SOURCE OF EXISTING POSITIVE REINFORCERS is the high probability or frequently performed behaviors or activities themselves. (They are called "high-probably behaviors because there is a high probably that they will be performed.) These may be actual work activities or leisure activities, but they must be activities or behaviors over which the person has discretion. Except for those who perform repetitive menial tasks, most employees have choices of which assignments they will work on at any given moment.

Brian, for example, is a secretary. He types memos, letters, short reports, and long reports; copies material; and files papers. Brian has considerable discretion in choosing when he will perform each task. Suppose that Brian generally types memos, letters, short reports first, leaving filing and typing long reports until last. Brian's typing memos, letters, and short reports can be considered, high-probability behaviors. Likewise, Brian's manager might observe that Brian drinks eight or nine cups of coffee each day and that during breaks he usually makes personal phone calls. These can considered high-probability leisure behaviors.

14

Manage Contingencies

CONTINGENCY MANAGEMENT STRATEGIES involve changing the if-then relationships between behavior and the consequences of those behaviors. Often, as we've seen, undesired behavior, such as gossiping, is reinforced while desired behavior, such as focused activity at one's desk, is ignored. The results of such dysfunctional contingencies is that gossiping increases while focused working declines. Intervention in these sorts of workplace dynamics involves changing the consequences to encourage the desired behaviors, such as getting the reports in on time, and to discourage undesired behaviors, like loafing and gossiping.

REARRANGE THE CONTINGENCIES

REARRANGING CONTINGENCIES the simplest intervention. Contingencies describe the behavior-consequence or if-then sequence. "*If* you work eight hours, *then* I will pay you." This statement describes the contingency relationship between work and pay. The "*then*-consequence" is contingent on the "*if*-behavior." Receiving payment is contingent on working eight hours.

The first step is to conduct a functional analysis to identify the ABCs (see Chapter 12) in order to discover the current contingencies, or the "if-then" relationship between the behavior and the consequences. Returning to Georgia and Otto, Georgia might discover that "If Otto makes a negative comment about the program, then I pay attention to him." She might also observe, "If Otto makes a negative comment about the program, then I react defensively." With these contingencies in play we would expect Otto's negative comments about the programs to continue and possibly to increase.

When the Undesired Behavior Is Rewarded

REARRANGING THE CONTINGENCIES means altering the if-then relationship so that the then-consequence follows a different if-behavior. For example, "If Otto makes a problem-solving comment, then I will pay attention to him; if he makes a negative comment about the program, then I will ignore him." Here, Georgia has rearranged the contingencies so that positive attention follows problem-solving comments while negative comments are ignored.

Ignore the undesirable behavior.
Notice the desirable behavior.

This strategy does not require adding anything new to the environment. It does not require new programs or bonuses or more money or more attention. Instead, the existing contingencies—the reinforcers and punishers—are simply rearranged.

When to Use

CONTINGENCY REARRANGEMENT IS MOST EFFECTIVE with undesirable behaviors that occur often and are reinforced by a positive consequence. A desirable behavior, such as problem-solving comments, is identified and substituted into the if-then statement. Usually the desirable behavior selected is one that is incompatible with the undesirable behavior.

> ## INCOMPATIBLE BEHAVIORS
>
> Two behaviors are said to be *incompatible* when they cannot be performed simultaneously. Examples of incompatible behaviors include: talking, being silent; sitting at desk, walking around; making a positive comment, making a negative comment; being on time, being late.

When the Reward Precedes the Desired Behavior

REARRANGEMENT OF CONTINGENCIES IS ALSO APPROPRIATE when the if-then sequence is out of order. Consider Jim's example: "Charlie has a really bad attitude, so I thought if I gave him a few breaks he'd shape up and be more committed. But it didn't work. Last week he wanted to take off a couple of hours early. I said it was OK with me if he got his sales log in the next afternoon. Well, I didn't see that log for four days!" This is a then-if sequence.

The contingencies need to be rearranged. The consequence must follow the behavior if it is to effectively increase that behavior. Jim's mistake was that he gave the reward before Charlie performed the desired behavior of getting in his completed sales log. This would be a little like the father saying to the child, you can eat your dessert now if you promise to eat your peas later. The consequence of getting off a couple of hours early must be made contingent on turning in the completed log sheet. The consequence of getting dessert must be contingent upon eating all peas first.

When the Desired Behavior Is Ignored or Punished

ANOTHER SITUATION in which contingency rearrangement is employed is when a desirable behavior, which occurs infrequently, is followed by no consequence or a negative one. For example, if Ralph is on time, then his supervisor ignores him. Or if Betty makes a suggestion, then her supervisor criticizes it. Ralph's on-time behavior is being extinguished and Betty's suggestions are being punished. In situations such as these the then-consequence needs to be changed from negative to positive.

Use Favored Work

THE PREMACK PRINCIPLE OF REINFORCEMENT states that a high-probability behavior can reinforce or reward a low-prob-ability behavior. In other words, doing something that we do often can reinforce doing something that we rarely do. For example, if an employee is more likely to leave his desk and go to the copy room to use the photocopy machine than he is to file folders, then going to the copy room can probably be used to reinforce filing folders.

Returning to Brian, if he tends to put off typing long reports and filing, his supervisor can assist him in being more productive by rearranging the contingencies and using work to reinforce work. The supervisor would rear-ranged the contingencies so that high-probabil-ity work behavior, such as Brian typing memos, letters, and short reports *after* performing the low-probability work behaviors of filing and typing long reports. The supervisor can consider any of Brian's high-probabil-ity behaviors (typing memos, letters, and short reports) as potential reinforc-ers to insert into an if-then statement. For example, if Brian types a long report, then he can type five letters. The Premack Principle is one of the most valuable and potent tools for supervisors because it uses work to reward work and costs nothing. It is not necessary to add anything new to the environment to increase performance.

When observing consequences of employee behavior, supervisors all too frequently discover to their dismay that there are few positive reinforcers in operation. This is common because most work environments are not very reinforcing. Rarely are supervisors deliberately punitive; rather they become punitive through frustration. Punishment gets immediate (although temporary) results so that a vicious cycle of being punished by the supervisor and working to avoid that punishment becomes entrenched.

CONTINGENCY ADDITION

IF YOU FIND THAT YOUR ENVIRONMENT has few existing reinforcers try contingency addition, which is also helpful when the problem behavior is maintained by intermittent reinforcement or when it consumes the reinforcer. The contingency addition strategy involves introducing more reinforcers into the environment. This is accomplished by increasing how often existing reinforcers are used or by identifying new reinforcers to insert into the if-then statement.

EXTINCTION AND PUNISHMENT AS CONTINGENT CONSEQUENCES

MANAGERS ROUTINELY EMPLOY contingency management principles, but unfortunately the contingencies are often punishment and extinction. "If you are late, then I will dock your pay, or "If you make a typo, then I will criticize you" are examples of if-then statements in which the then-consequence is punishment. "If you are on time then I will ignore you," or "If you correct all the typos, then I will say nothing" are examples of if-then statements in which the then-consequence is no response which leads to extinction.

Obviously managers don't intend to ignore desired performance. It's another example of how focusing on the problem—the undesirable behavior—entraps managers in a

Changing your focus is like switching glasses.

punitive cycle. We all do it. It is the seduction of negativity. We become ensnared in the struggle to squelch a problem which blinds us. Skilled people handlers, like coaches and personal trainers, override their natural tendency to focus on reducing the problem by *mindfully looking to the positive.* This is best accomplished by identifying a desirable behavior to be increased rather than an undesirable behavior to be decreased.

Accomplishing this change of focus is like switching glasses so that you can view the situation through a difference lens. This technique of purposefully changing perspective is called "reframing."

Ignore the Undesired Behavior

WHEN THE PROBLEM BEHAVIOR HAS BEEN TRANSLATED into a desired behavior to increase, use a combination of reinforcement plus extinction as the contingent consequences. For example, Instead of "If you are on-time, then I will say nothing because you are suppose to be on time. If you are late I will criticize you", change your focus to the desired behavior with "If you are on time, then I will extend friendly good morning greeting; if you are late, then I will say nothing."

Extinction is almost always preferable to punishment. Extinction or the reduction in the frequency of a behavior occurs when behavior has no consequence. Thus, the best strategy is to ignore the undesirable behavior which promotes extinction, and to reinforce an desirable incompatible behavior. When employed systematically, this strategy will effectively increase the frequency of the desired behavior and avoid the negative side effects of punishment.

Many managers feel that employees "should" work and feel that they shouldn't have to acknowledge employees' appropriate behavior. They say, "He gets paid to work. Why should I have reward him too?" The assumption is that the paycheck is rewarding and therefore the boss has fulfilled his obligations. Considering the paycheck in terms of reinforcement principles. The paycheck is received for

It is easy to get caught up in "shoulds". being present at the job site a certain number of hours, not for doing efficient work. In fact, the person may not actually work all of the time, but may goof off—and get paid for it!

Many managers have difficulty ignoring problem behavior in order to focus on productive behavior. With a chronically late employee, for example, they say, "She knows she's *supposed* to be on time—I just can't say nothing when she comes in late!" It is easy to get caught up in "shoulds". Managers often fear that if the smallest error goes unmentioned it will spread like a malignancy. Science shows that just the opposite is true. Innumerable studies have demonstrated that long-term behavior changes are most effectively accomplished through positive reinforcement plus extinction (ignoring the problem behavior).

It is easier to understand when you view the employee in the context of the environment and ask the question: "What consequences are maintaining this undesirable behavior?" Sometimes the punishment is actually keeping the problem going. In an environment with little reinforcement, negative attention can become reinforcing. In other situations, negative attention may be perceived as positive ("Boy, did I get her goat that time! Hah!"). The best testimonial is experience. By abandoning punitive consequences and substituting extinction plus reinforcement, you are less likely to promote avoidance while nonproductive emotional reactions, such as anger, fear, and crying, that are a common side effect of punishment, will be less frequent.

When the Problem Can't Be Ignored

THERE MAY BE SITUATIONS when you believe that it is imperative that you comment on substandard performance. When you can not ignore the problem behavior, confront the employee in a way that is not punitive-that is, avoid evaluation or criticism. Begin by describing the substandard performance, then express your concern that the behavior be brought up to standards and ask for suggestions to improve performance. Finally, negotiate a contingency contract, which is an explicit agreed upon if-then interaction.

TASC Plus provides a step-by-step process for guiding this sort of coaching. For example, when coaching you might say the following to a salesman who has failed to meet his quota: "Ben, you closed seven deals last week. I am concerned about this, because the quota is sixteen. (Tell) What suggestions do you have for increasing your sales? (Ask)" Use any reasonable suggestion as a starting point for negotiating a change plan (Specify). State what benefit will come as a result of increased sales (Consequence).

There are times when punishment might be the most appropriate conse- quence, but such instances are few. If the undesirable behavior is a threat to people or to property (such as driving a forklift too fast around the yard), punish- ment in the form of a reprimand would be appropriate. But punishment should always be used in combina- tion with reinforcement. Punish the undesirable behavior of driving the forklift too fast and reinforce the desirable behavior of driving the forklift slowly.

Punishment usually results in immediate cessation of the punished behavior, *but it does not teach or encourage a desirable behavior.*

When the forklift driver stops speeding, how he does drive is left to chance. Further, punishment does not result in lasting change, in most cases. By using punishment in combination with rein- forcement, you create a hiatus in the performance of undesirable behavior because the punishment tends to suppress it momen- tarily. This is your opportunity to use reinforce a more appropri- ate behavior.

Improving Clerk Performance
by Managing the Contingencies

THE OWNER OF A NEIGHBORHOOD GROCERY STORE was having problems with two clerks. Industrial psychologists helped the owner specify the problems in terms of desired behaviors to be increased. Three behavior categories were identified: the location of the clerks in the store, the speed and nature of assistance given to customers, and the quantity of merchandise on the shelves.

COUNTER-PRODUCTIVE PATTERN

A FUNCTIONAL ANALYSIS to determine what was preventing the desired behaviors from occurring revealed a general pattern of negative reinforcement. When the clerks did not perform as expected, the owner nagged them, so that the nagging became an antecedent that prompted work. The consequence to clerks for working was that the owner *stopped nagging*. Exactly what was expected of the clerks was never made explicit, however.

CHANGE PLAN

TO ALTER THIS COUNTERPRODUCTIVE PATTERN, the psychologists began by pinpointing the specific behaviors and outcomes expected: "When any customer requests assistance, the assistance should begin within five seconds of the request." To establish baseline on the frequency of pinpointed behaviors and outcomes, data was collected during four 15-minute observation periods scheduled at different times during the day (time sampling). Finally, positive consequences— feedback from the observer, self-recording by the clerks of their own performance to prompt self-reinforcement, and contingent time off with pay— were used as reinforcers instead of the negative consequence of the owner's stopping his nagging.

PHASE-IN

THE CHANGE PROGRAM DID NOT FOCUS on all behaviors immediately. Location of clerks was the target of the first phase. Increasing the quality of customer service was added a week later, followed in the third week by an increase in the quantity of merchandise available for sale. At the beginning of each of the phases, the pinpointed behaviors and outcomes were explained and demonstrated to the clerks. When, necessary, clerks rehearsed the pinpointed behavior. Clerks were given a checklist for self-monitoring and were instructed to record results each time a school bell was sounded. The ringing of the bell eight times a day served as an antecedent to prompt self-recording. A graph depicting the baseline was posted. Clerks were told that whenever they engaged in the behaviors at a frequency of 90 percent or more (assigned goal), they would be rewarded by getting time off with pay.

PERFORMANCE IMPROVED

THE PROGRAM EVALUATION substantiated three things. First, the program worked as was hoped—the level of performance for each behavior increased significantly: Appropriate location of clerks went from an average of 53 to 86 percent; speed of customer assistance, from average of 35 to 87 percent; and quantity of groceries on the shelves, from an average of 57 to 86 percent.

Second, the frequency of pinpointed behaviors increased only after the proper intervention was introduced. During the first phase, the amount of time the clerks spent in the store increased, but their speed of assisting customers and of keeping the shelves filled did not. (These other pinpointed behaviors increased only after they had become the focus of the change program.)

Third, the evaluation demonstrated that the clerks accurately recorded their performance: A comparison revealed observers' and clerks' recordings to be almost identical.

OWNER TRAINED TO MAINTAIN

THE CLERKS' BEHAVIOR CHANGED when the psychologist changed the contingencies. But steps must be taken to maintain the improvement afterwards, otherwise the clerks will likely drift back to their old habits. Behavioral change programs are designed to bring about change by manipulating the environment in a structured way. Interventions are short term and are not meant to be ongoing programs. Ideally, one result is setting up an ecological system whereby factors in the environment continue to prompt and reinforce a high frequency of the desired behavior.

To accomplish this in the grocery store, the researchers focused on the owner as the maintenance agent. During baseline and intervention phases, the owner frequently served as the second observer. Through this process, he learned how to observe and to give feedback. The owner was also trained to praise or otherwise to reinforce clerks when he saw them performing as desired. After 12 weeks, when the formal program ended, the owner was able to maintain the clerks' behavior at or close to the 90 percent criterion with a combination of feedback, praise, and contingent paid time off. Presumably, the owner's behavior was maintained by increased profits and by an improvement in the clerks' performance.

15

Negotiate Performance Contracts

A Performance contract is an explicit agreement between you and the employee that specifies the if-then agreement—the behavior to be performed and the contingencies that will result. Change programs almost always involve an alteration of current contingencies. An employee who is not aware of the program may become confused when the contingencies suddenly change. Contracting can help eliminate this confusion: By working out the contract with the employee during the coaching, you have access to valuable feedback. By listening and incorporating the feedback, you encourage cooperation and are more likely to get a genuine commitment from the employee. When the target person knows and agrees to the contingencies, the change process is accelerated.

NEGOTIATED AGREEMENT

Many managers use informal agreements in their coaching sessions, but frequently they fail to produce the desire change. "If you improve your attitude, then you'll get ahead around here" is one example. Such a "contract" does not specify exactly what behaviors are expected. The employee may have a very differ set of behaviors in mind from those the manager desires. Likewise, the contract does not specify exactly what the contingency is. What does "to get ahead" mean? Is it a promotion? More money? More priviledges? Disappointment and confusion can be avoided with the contingencies are spelled out in the contract.

If

THE FIRST STEP IS TO PINPOINT THE "IF" PORTION of the contract. These elements should be included in pinpointing: (1) specific behavior—what; (2) the situation where the behavior is to be performed—where, when, with whom; and (3) the amount of the behavior expected—how much, how long. There should be no ambiguity in any of these elements.

Then

THE SECOND STEP IS TO DETERMINE THE "THEN" PORTION of contract. An appropriate reinforcer must be identified and agreed on. Again, it is important to be very specific. If the contingency involves a response from you, then state explicitly what you agree to do or say. If the contingency is an activity that the employee can engage in (such as making a personal call), clearly describe that activity well as the amount. Through contingency contracting, the manager teaches employees to better manage their own work behavior.

Determine Consequences

HIGH-PROBABILITY BEHAVIORS ARE IDEAL REINFORCERS for contingency contracts in organizational settings. That is, behaviors that the person is already performing can be used as reinforcers. These generally include work activities and leisure activities. For example, "after you make one call to a new client, then you may make five calls to current clients." In this contract, a high-probability work behavior, calling current clients, is contingent on a low-probability work behavior, calling a new client. "When you type six letters without errors, then you may make one five-minute personal call." Here a high-probability leisure behavior is used as the contingent reinforcer. Notice that in both cases the amount of the activity is clearly indicated.

Fair & Honest

THE CONTRACT MUST BE FAIR and the behavior expected should be one that the employee can reasonably perform. Contracts that require people to perform behaviors they don't know well or that require a substantial increase in frequency generally fail, whereas contracts that specify a small increase in the frequency of a familiar behavior are more successful.

The contract must be honest. Contingencies should be carried out immediately and within the terms of the contract. If for some reason the agreed upon contingencies cannot be delivered, negotiate a new contract with the person. A series of short-term contracts, such as a week or a month long, is generally better than a long-term one, like six months or a year. The duration of the contract should be definite, not open-ended. The expiration date is an opportunity to review progress and revise the contract's terms. The contract's terms should be clear, in writing, and be signed by you and by the target person. Signing the contract adds to clarity and emphasizes the commitment on both sides.

Seek Win–Win Plan

MEETING THE NEEDS of both supervisor and employee is essential. The contract that fails to meet one or the other's needs will probably fail to change the problem behavior. Carrying out the terms of the contract would not be reinforcing to that person.

Many supervisors react to contingency contracting as "bribery," but it can just as easily be viewed as a structured method of setting up a win-win interaction. The structure reduces trial and error and facilitates success.

Encourages Self-Direction

CONTINGENCY CONTRACTING IS A POWERFUL MANAGEMENT TOOL in promoting self-directed work behavior. By using the contracting method to solve behavior problems, you simultaneously teach employees to manage their own behavior more effectively. The ideal goal is a setting in which all employees develop and carry out contracts with themselves and with others. You can teach and reinforce employee self-directed behavior by gradually shifting the determining role from yourself to the employee. This involves moving from manager-controlled contracting to employee-controlled contracting. In manager-controlled contracting, you determine the amount of the task required and the amount of the reinforcer to be given. When the employee performs the task, you deliver the reinforcement. As the employee better understand the process, give that individual the responsibility for determining behavior and consequences and for delivering the reinforcer. If you do this systematically and consistently, you can increase self-directed work behavior. The reward to you is a more productive team and more time for other aspects of your work.

16

Special Challenges

There are two situations when contingency rearrangement is difficult to use. These are when the behavior consumes the reinforcement and when the reinforcement is intermittent.

CONSUMMATORY BEHAVIOR

WHEN THE PROBLEM BEHAVIOR is maintained by a reinforcer that is consumed by the employee, it is not usually possible to rearrange the contingencies because the reinforcement cannot be separated from the behavior. Drinking too much at lunch and making frequent personal phone calls are

examples. Each sip of the cocktail is immediately reinforced by the alcohol and the pleasure of chatting with the friend reinforces the personal call.

The easiest kind of intervention is one in which you alter the consequences. But in order to do that, you have to be able to provide a new consequence for the target behavior. Unfortunately, it isn't always possible to separate the reinforcement from the behavior, such as what happens when behaviors consume the reinforcer. For example, smoking is reinforced by inhaling the smoke; overeating is reinforced by ingesting food; too many drinks at lunch by the drinks themselves; talking on the phone by the verbal responses and the pleasure of chatting.

With such consummatory behaviors you can easily identify the consequence, but rarely change it because you can't separate that behavior from its reinforcing consequence. Thus when the target behavior is consummatory you need to look to the antecedent for a clue as to how to modify that behavior.

INTERMITTENT CONSEQUENCES

THE SECOND CHALLENGE is when the undesired behavior is intermittently reinforced, it is resistant to extinction. Because intermittent reinforcers occur so infrequently, it is difficult to identify the reinforcers so that they can be rearranged.

Intermittent reinforcement and avoidance behaviors obscure identification of consequences maintaining problem behaviors because the behavior occurs many times without reinforcement. In these cases, uncovering antecedents is essential to understanding how the problem behavior functions.

Some behaviors are resistant to extinction because they are maintained on an intermittent schedule of reinforcement. In other words, the behavior goes without consequences—is unreinforced—many times, but continues because there is an occasional reinforcement.

Intermittent reinforcers are difficult to identify. If the problem behavior is reinforced only one time in ten occurrences, you must observe the behavior 30 times just to obtain three examples of the consequence. Reliable conclusions cannot be drawn from only three examples. Obviously, such lengthy observation is not generally feasible in the workplace.

AVOIDANCE

THE CONSEQUENCES OF AVOIDANCE are even more difficult to
identify. An avoidance behavior is performed to avoid some
punishing consequence. If it is successful in avoiding
punishment, then the punishing consequence does not
occur. If the punishment doesn't occur, it can't be observed. Yet, with avoidance behavior there *is a consequence*—avoidance of punishment, which is a positive
consequence. Remember that turning off or avoiding
punishment is negative reinforcement. That is, it is rewarding by virtue of avoiding pain. It is the "it-feels-so-good-
when-it-stops" type of reward.

CAMEO OF NEGATIVE REINFORCEMENT

A man is banging his head against the wall. A
second man asks, "Why are you banging your
head against that wall? The first man answers, "Because it feels so good when I stop".

Sometimes, by imagining what would happen if a person
were to perform differently in certain situation, you can
guess at the consequence that is being avoided. If one of
the possible consequences turns out to be punishing, this
suggests that the target behavior is an avoidance behavior.
For example, when the radio station manager asked Charles
what would happen if he were to ask Rosemary directly for
the projection, Charles said, "She'd just ask a bunch of
questions and make me defend every decision I made!"
Because Charles stated this in a way that suggested it was
punishing to him, his manager could suspect that Charles's
procrastination was tied to his avoidance of directing
Rosemary.

Look for the Antecedents

WITH AVOIDANCE we must look to the antecedent to get a
handle on what controls the problem behavior. If the
problem behavior is successful in avoiding something

negative, then the person is likely to engage in that same
problem behavior in similar situations. The situation that
triggered the avoidance is the antecedent. So with avoidance behaviors, you need to study the situation and events
in play *just before* the avoidance occurred.

HOW TO DISCOVER ANTECEDENTS

WHEN A STIMULUS IS PRESENTED each time a behavior is reinforced, that antecedent stimulus eventually gains the
power to evoke the behavior. Likewise, when a behavior is
repeatedly punished in the presence of a particular stimulus, that stimulus soon becomes associated with punishment and signals to the person that punishment is immi-
nent. If the person avoids punishment, the stimulus can
become an antecedent that triggers future avoidance

FUNCTIONAL ANALYSIS OF OTTO'S BEHAVIOR

A Antecedent	B Behavior	C Consequence
Mentioned new responsibilities in innovative program.	Otto questioned necessity of the innovative program.	Told Otto why innovative program is necessary.
Discussed sales promotion under innovative program.	Otto said promotion wouldn't work	Told Otto I had a lot of experience.
Discussed procedures for keeping records in innovative program.	Otto said old method was a lot better and cheaper.	reminded Otto that I am the manager.

behavior. Each time the person avoids the punishment, the antecedent becomes more powerful in its ability to evoke avoidance behavior. Because antecedents can become very powerful in turning behaviors on and off, it is important that these cues be identified.

To discover antecedents, the events that occur *just before* the target behavior must be identified and recorded. When several examples have been collected, the next step is to look for a common theme. Consider Melody, who makes personal calls during work time. Her supervisor observed that Melody frequently made a phone call after she finished typing an assignment. Here the antecedent that evoked the consummatory behavior of making phone calls was probably finishing an assignment.

When you have difficulty identifying what occurs just before the behavior in question, a complete description of the situation may reveal the antecedent. When Georgia wrote a complete description of the situation in which Otto's problem behavior occurred, she discovered the antecedent: "Whenever I mention my innovative program in the weekly staff meeting, Otto makes negative comments about the program." This description suggests that the antecedent of Otto's negative commenting is "mention of the innovative program." And indeed, when Georgia carefully recorded each instance of Otto's negative comments in one staff meeting, she confirmed this observation. After each mention of the innovative program Otto made a negative comment. Here is Georgia's functional analysis of Otto's behavior.

17

Use
Stimulus Control

STIMULI PRESENT WHEN BEHAVIOR IS REINFORCED or punished can become powerful cues that inform the person of the probable consequence of a behavior. Your presence, for example, can become a cue that signals that looking busy will have positive consequences and loafing will have negative ones. Rarely does a person deliberate over such processes, instead the antecedent is perceived and the behavior is performed without thought. The antecedent becomes such a powerful a cue that it "controls" the behavior. Behavioral psychologists call this "stimulus control."

Work behavior can be brought under stimulus control by arranging the conditions in such a way that a particular work is associated with a particular antecedent cue. Consider Bill's problem. One of Bill's responsibilities was to write proposals. In his previous position he wrote many proposals with little trouble. But in his new position he arrived each morning determined to write, only to find that he had difficulty getting started and could work on the proposal for only a few minutes before feeling paralyzed. He entered office and sat at his desk with the intention of writing. But while sitting at the desk he engaged in several other behaviors, such as answering his mail, talking on the phone, reading the paper, reviewing resource material, eating lunch, and chatting with peers. Many of these behaviors were reinforced, so that sitting at his desk lost much of its power as an antecedent to proposal writing. In a sense his desk had become contaminated as a stimulus for working.

Bill's supervisor understood the power of stimulus control. He suggested that Bill move his work station into the conference room where Bill would do nothing but write. If he began to daydream, for example, he was to leave the area. If he wanted to take a break he was to leave the area. Eventually writing came under stimulus control-that is, entering the conference room evoked or signaled writing. As Bill employed this technique he found find it easier and easier to write in the conference room.

Of course, it is essential that the writing in the conference room be reinforced. The act of writing itself and seeing the words on the paper, as well as the feeling of accomplishment they evoke, were reinforcing, but it would be wise for Bill's supervisor to insure reinforcement with contingency contracting, such as "After I write in the conference room for 30 minutes, then I may open the mail." In this contract writing (behavior) in the conference room (antecedent) is reinforced by the high-probability behavior of opening the mail (consequence). A word of caution: Bill should not attempt to begin by going into the conference room and trying to write for two or three hours; instead he should start off by requiring himself to write for only a short time in the begin-

ning. The length of time is then gradually increased.

AVOID CONTAMINATION

THE LACK OF STIMULUS CONTROL can create problems in all areas of the company. In small offices, for example, employees frequently engage in a lot of socializing. This reduces the stimulus control power of the office, so that the socializing undermines productivity. Socializing can be controlled without punishment by designating a specific area for its occurrence and then setting a time limit on breaks. In general, arrange for a situation or a signal to be associated wit the behaviors that you want to encourage. It is easier to establish an association between a new antecedent and a desired work behavior than it is to revitalize an antecedent that has become contaminated by its association with several undesirable behaviors.

CREATE GENERALIZATION

THERE ARE TIMES when you do not want the performance of a behavior restricted to one situation. Training is a prime example. Time and money is poorly invested if skills learned in training workshops are not generalized to the entire work environment. Yet all too often this important step is neglected. Let's examine this problem more closely.

Stimulus generalization occurs when a behavior that has been learned in the presence of one antecedent is performed in the presence of other, similar antecedents. The more similar the subsequent antecedents are to the original one, the more likely the behavior will be performed. Training sessions should therefore employ mock settings and situations that resemble the work setting in which the behavior is to be performed. Whenever possible, training should move out of the workshop into the target setting. The more the training approximates the target setting, the more generalization can be expected.

Assign Practice Tasks

Whether it's training or your individual coaching, when you work with employees in developing skills, homework assignments are a valuable tool. For example, in the first session of my communications skills workshop, I teach questioning techniques for gathering information. During the workshop session, participants practice the techniques in small groups. As a homework assignment, they are requested to conduct a "shyness poll" in which they interview three people about their experiences with shyness. In additions to learning first hand that most people have felt shy, they practice their interviewing skills in a situation outside the workshop setting. As they do their assignments, stimulus generalization begins to occur. If the behavior meets with positive consequences, they are more likely to perform the behavior again outside the workshop.

Any training can include assignments that require participants to perform the new skills in their work settings. For example, participants in sales training could be asked to tape record an actual sales pitch, which they can review with the trainer to receive valuable feedback. In short, training is incomplete if it ends in the classroom. To be effective, the training must be structured to move from the classroom into the target environment.

18

Use Shaping

BEHAVIOR CHANGE PROGRAMS depend heavily on reinforcement of a desired behavior. This means that the employee must first perform the behavior so that you can reinforce it. You can not expect people to perform a behavior that they do not know how to perform, however. A behavior that an employee does not now possess much be learned, because new and complex behaviors rarely emerge spontaneously.

The lack of shaping is one of the most common reasons for failure in behavior change programs. Shaping requires that you accept as adequate performance that is not perfect but an approximation of the desired behavior. Then, slow improvements are rewarded as the employee learns to perform as desired.

Any change program that calls for an increase in a behavior should use some shaping. Too frequently, however, managers hold out for perfect performance, which greatly decreases the chance that the behavior will ever occur. To effectively teach a new behavior, you must reinforce approximations that may be much lower that the desired behavior and proceed step by step as the behavior slowly improves.

This is how a child learns to speak, for example. At first the child

Don't wait for perfect performance.

Forget shoulds; work with what is. makes guttural noises and cooing. When some of these noises resemble words, the parents gush praises. Over time, however, the parents expect words to be articulated more clearly before praising the child. Then the parents expect strings of words, then full sentences before praising, and so forth.

Some managers believe that employees "should" per-form at certain standards and do not "deserve" to be reinforced for performance that is below that standard. Managers who have this attitude impede learning because they don't reinforce important progress in the learning process leading to meeting the standard.

To help employees learn a new behavior, even if it is one that they should already know, begin positive attention at whatever level at which the employee is currently performing and slowly but steadily move toward the goal, reinforcing small progress steps.

BEGIN AT BASELINE

THIS IS AN ADDITIONAL REASON for having a good baseline. Baseline tells us the current level of performance, which is where the shaping process should begin. Reinforce the employee for per-forming at the baseline level or slightly above it. Call this step one. When the employee consis-tently carries out the behavior at that level, move upward one small step. Now the employee must perform at step two to gain the reinforcer previously given for step one. Shaping continues in this manner until the employee reaches the goal.

The shaping process can never begin at too low a level and the steps can never be too small.

Whenever you are in doubt, begin at a lower step or reduce the size of the steps. Make it *easy* for the person to perform the desired behavior. This is important because it increases your chances of success. First steps especially must be very small and easily attainable in order to create a movement. Success in mastering the first steps can be reinforcing in and of itself, adding to the momentum. Once the employee is moving, the later steps can be progressively larger. Frustration and failure in beginning steps acts as a brake, which makes progress a slow, laborious process that is hardly reinforcing.

The Shaping Continuum

A TENTATIVE SERIES OF STEPS should be determined at the onset of the shaping program. The follow schedule was developed to improve the performance of a quality control checker in training.

Baseline: 18 defective units passed a day

Goal: 2 or fewer defective units passed a day.

Step 1   For one week 17 or fewer defective units passed per day.

Step 2   For one week 15 or fewer defective units passed per day.

Step 3   For one week 12 or fewer defective units passed per day.

Step 4   For one week 8 or fewer defective units passed per day.

Step 5   For one week 4 or fewer defective units passed per day.

Step 6   2 or fewer defective units passed per day.

Small steps. Steps planned on paper may seem easier than they really are so that the size of steps may need to be reduced. Be flexible and ready to change the schedule. The employee may have to work on one step for several time periods, or may have to return to an earlier step if a setback occurs. It is important to establish a pattern of success. So as a rule of thumb move up a step only after the previous objective has been met.

The schedule with the quality control checker is designed to shape behavior by increasing the amount of the target behavior, which is the number of defective units spotted. Many schedules are built along a time continuum in which each subsequent step in the shaping requires that the person perform the behavior for a longer time than the previous step to achieve the objective. Bill, the man who couldn't concentrate on his proposal writing, could follow a schedule that increased the amount of time he was to spend writing at each step, for example.

Schedules can also be developed around the chain of behaviors necessary to produce the goal behavior. A schedule for Arlene could specify a chain of behaviors as follows: (1) analyze the problem, (2) generate solutions, (3) implement solutions without assistance. Of course, each step should be broken down into a series of smaller substeps.

SET STEP-BY-STEP OBJECTIVES

EACH STEP IN SHAPING SHOULD BE CLEARLY DEFINED. Each shaping step should be stated in terms of an objective. State objectives in terms of the behaviors to be carried out. This signals when one shaping step has been successfully achieved and when the next step should begin.

Pinpoint the behavior in such a way that it can be counted so that you can establish a baseline. Specify the situation where the behavior is to occur and the amount of the behavior required.

Consider the following objectives:

OBJECTIVE 1: "**For one week Arlene will work more independently.**" An objective stated like this one will surely result in failure. What is independent work? Because the behavior Arlene is expected to perform is not clearly defined, it will probably lead to erratic reinforcement of a variety of behaviors. Furthermore, on what is Arlene to work independently and for how long? Is one instance of independent work sufficient to satisfy the objective? This ambiguity sets Arlene up for failure and frustration.

OBJECTIVE 2: "**For one week Arlene will make more suggestions for solutions.**" This objective is an improvement. A statement that suggests a solution can be counted so that you know what to reinforce. But the objective fails to specify the nature of the suggested solutions. Do suggestions as to where to go to lunch satisfy the objective? And the objective fails to specify how many suggestions are required.

OBJECTIVE 3: "**For one week when Arlene asks me to assist her with one of her assignments, she will make at least two suggestions for solutions to her problem.**" This statement meets all the criteria for a behavioral objective. It defines the behavior—suggestions for solutions to her problem; it defines the circumstances—when Arlene asks for assistance with her assignments; and it specifies how much—at least two suggestions.

A good objective tells you, the manager, exactly what to pay attention to (reinforce) and it helps the employee to know what to do and when. When the employee participates in the change process—and this should be most of the time—each objective can be converted into a contingency contract that specifies the objective in the "if" portion and the reinforcement in the "then" portion. "If you make two suggestions for solutions to your problems when you ask me for assistance on your assignments, then I will listen to each suggestions and comment on its merits."

How To Identify Steps

THE BEST WAY TO IDENTIFY THE SHAPING STEPS needed in a chain is to begin with the goal behavior or outcome and, working backwards, identify each behavior that is necessary to complete the subsequent step.

Of each step, ask the question: "Can the employee do this now?" If the answer is "No", then ask, "What does she need to do first?" When you can answer "Yes" you have identified where to begin the shaping steps.

Returning to Arlene, the backward analysis might go like this. "Can Arlene implement solutions without assistance now? If no, then what must she do first?" Arlene must be able to implement solutions with assistance before she can implement then without assistance. "Can Arlene implement solutions with assistance now? If no, what must she do first?" Before Arlene can implement solutions she must generate potential solutions. "Can Arlene generate solutions now? If no, what must she do first?" Before Arlene can generate solutions, she must first analyze the problem. "Can Arlene analyze the problem now? If no, what must she do first?' And so forth until we identify Arlene's level of ability. Then each of these behavioral steps to implementing solutions without assistance can be shaped through a similar series of small steps.

When Improvement Plateaus

PLATEAUING IS A COMMON OCCURRENCE in the course of a shaping. An employee may make excellent progress and then lose momentum. When this happens you can prompt new movement by reducing the size of the steps. Increasing the reinforcement after each successfully completed might also help.

ARRANGE FOR PRACTICE

IN "BEHAVIORAL REHEARSAL" OR PRACTICE, the person rehearses the role or behaviors that he or she wishes to learn and is reinforced for successful performance at each link in the chain of behaviors. It is vital that you use shaping during the rehearsal—that is, that you reinforce approximations of the desired behavior rather than waiting for a perfect performance. The easiest way to do this is to give plentiful positive feedback on what the person did well and with a minimum of so-called "constructive criticism." Focus on successive approximations of the desired behavior rather and ignore the undesired behavior.

Gradually make the rehearsal setting more and more like the target setting. If this is not done, the person may learn to perform the behavior in the rehearsal setting, such as your office, but not outside it, such as on the sales floor. By making the setting increasingly realistic, you assist in generalizing the learning.

Shape up one class of behaviors at a time during the rehearsal. For example, in teaching assertive behaviors, first shape the words, then the voice quality and control, then the body movements, and finally all of them together. Try it—it's easy, it's free, and you can shape up your management skills when you participate in the rehearsal.

The more real and believable the model, the better.

MODELING

SOMETIMES THE EMPLOYEE WILL NOT KNOW how to perform the first step. Using a model can solve this problem. Modeling is learning indirectly by watching others perform. We learn vicariously what behaviors will be reinforced or punished by observing or hearing about another's performance. Modeling includes demonstrations of behavior, pictures and descriptions in books, and oral reports. Viewing a live or filmed model is best because we can observe exactly how the behavior is performed, the exact sequences of behaviors, and the consequences of each.

Arrange Modeling Opportunities

EVEN WHEN AN EMPLOYEE is not actively involved in the shaping program, you can still employ models to encourage the manifestation of certain behaviors. Suppose that you want

Modeling occurs constantly. to shape an employee's assertive behavior, without her being aware of your efforts. One strategy is to reinforce another employee's assertive behavior in the presence of the employee in question. Through observation, the person will learn assertive behaviors and their consequences, but may still not act assertively. Perhaps she needs to be prompted, such as "Ann, I'd be interested in your opinion on this topic." Then you would reinforce any assertive response. Suppose the person says, "Gee, I really don't know." You can redefine this reply as an assertive response and reinforce it: "I'm glad you could say that. Maybe we should take a second look before coming to a conclusion. What questions do you still have?"

Credibility

SOME MODELS ARE BETTER THAN OTHERS. The more real and believable the model, the better. As a general guideline, the model should have credibility and status in the target employee's eyes. Less learning occurs when the model's credibility is discounted, but some learning still occurs. The model should also have the person's respect, and it is best if the model is a member of the person's current group or of the group to which the person aspires.

Use With Other Interventions

MODELS CAN BE USED in any of the intervention strategies. From models we learn how to perform the behavior, what consequences to expect, as well as in what situation to perform it. The important thing to remember is that modeling occurs constantly. When you reinforce an employee's behavior, you increase the probability that that person—and all those watching—will perform that behavior in the future. Similarly, when you punish an employee, you "set an example", and observers are less likely to engage in the undesirable behavior. But punishment can produce counterproductive side effects, which means that any or all of those who learned from the example are more likely to sabotage, steal, engage in angry outbursts, become overly anxious, or withdraw.

19

Use Tokens

Tokens are objects that take on reinforcing value because they can be exchanged for a tangible reinforcement. Money is a token, for example. The coins and paper have no inherent value but can be used to purchase an unlimited variety of reinforcers.

ADVANTAGES

There are several advantages to tokens. Because they can be converted into a variety of reinforcers, they allow for individualized reinforcement. For example, a company might give employees points for being time, and such points can be accumulated and exchanged for items in a mail-order catalogue. Points allow all employees involved to select rewards of their own choice.

Another advantage is that the tokens and points bridge the delay between the time employees perform as desired and when they actually receive the reward. In theory, the Christmas bonus is supposed to reinforce quality work in the past year, but because the bonus comes so

long after the performance of the work behavior, its reinforcing power is greatly reduced. In contrast, points can be given almost immediately for a variety of desirable work behaviors, and these points can then be accumulated and exchanged for a individually tailored bonus. In this system, even though the bonus comes only once a year its reinforcing value extends throughout the year as the employee earns the points.

Flexible

WITH A TOKEN SYSTEM, those who have exhibited superior performance earn more points than do those whose performance is average. This makes the bonus truly contingent, because you simply insert a specific number of points into the if-then statement. "If you complete the report on time, then you will receive three points." This allows you to use the same reinforcer—the points—with several people as well as to reinforce several different behaviors of one person.

It is not necessary that a token or point system be company-wide. It can be established in a single office, division, or with a single employee. Points can be exchanged for a variety of reinforcers, such extended lunch hours or additional breaks. The token system works well in conjunction with the reinforcement menu discussed below. A final advantage is that tokens can be used in conjunction with shaping to increase behavior slowly by gradually requiring more and more performance of the behavior to earn a token or point.

USING TOKENS TO
INCREASING PUNCTUALITY

ANNUAL BONUSES proved ineffective increasing punctuality and attendance in bathroom fixtures manufacturing plant in Mexico City. Likewise, disciplinary interviews and one-day suspensions without pay failed to reduce tardiness. A token program was implemented with six chronically tardy semiskilled male laborers. The system was simple: Each day that the worker punched in on time or earlier, he was given a slip of paper stating that he had earned approximately two pesos. At the end of each week, the men went to the Supervisor of Industrial Relations and exchanged their slips for cash. Statistical analysis revealed a significant decrease in tardiness when the incentive program was in effect.

REINFORCEMENT TECHNIQUES

THIS PROGRAM EMPLOYED a number of reinforcement techniques. Most notable is that a small and more frequent (once a week) monetary reinforcement was substituted for a larger, less frequent (once a year) one. From learning theory we know that the shorter the time between the reinforcement and the behavior, the more power the reinforcement exerts over that behavior. The slips of paper, which functioned as tokens, closed the time gap even more. As soon as the worker performed the desired behavior of punching in on time or before the required time, he was reinforced with a token. The Supervisor of Industrial Relations, who conducted the study, probably also reinforced the workers with praise or smiles when they exchanged their slips.

EVALUATION

TWO PROCEDURES WERE FOLLOWED to evaluate the program. First, data on tardiness rates were collected for six workers who had similar tardiness patterns but did not receive incentives. Tardiness among these control workers averaged 9.8 percent over the 77 weeks of the study. In contrast, the average rate for target workers when incentives were being administered was less than 2 percent. The second control for comparison was the target workers themselves. The study used a reversal design in which the target workers were used as their own controls. After the baseline period, the incentive program was implemented and discontinued (reversed) three times. This procedure allowed a comparison between tardiness rates when the program was in effect and when it was not. There were three incentive periods and two reversals.

CONCLUSIONS

THE RESULTS POINT TO TWO CONCLUSIONS: First, reinforcing workers who punched in on time increased punctuality; second, behavior that was not reinforced stopped being performed. That workers knew what was expected of them and were capable of performing appropriately was substantiated by the increase in punctuality when the incentive program went into effect. Yet, when reinforcement for being on time was stopped, the workers stopped performing the desired behavior.

It should also be noted that the workers were reinforced for punching in on time. The incentive did not reinforce starting work on time. One could argue that if the workers were in the factory on time they were more likely to begin working on time, but this leaves performance of the desired behavior to chance. To be effective, the reinforcement should be linked to the desired behavior. To increase beginning work promptly, incentives might have been given for being at the work station and beginning work on time.

Always link reinforcement to the desired behavior.

Another interesting result was that although the rate of tardiness was reduced, the length of a tardy period did not change. In other words, there was no reinforcement for being less late. Incentives for a reduction in the length of lateness would be expected to reduce the average length of tardiness.

R+ MENU WOULD HELP

THE DIFFERENCE IN TARDY RATES between the target workers was interesting. During the three incentive periods, percentage rates for the least tardy worker were 0, 2, and 1.2 compared with 6.2, 5.6, and 5.4 for the most tardy worker. This difference indicates that the power of the incentive as a reinforcer was not the same for the two workers. Other reinforcers—such as longer breaks, cigarettes, or praise—might have been more effective than money in motivating the most tardy worker to get to work on time. Many behavior change programs employed in industrial settings neglect to tailor reinforcement to the individual. Of course, tailoring is difficult when using an incentive program with several dozen people. One way to solve this problem is the reinforcement menu technique in which the worker selects one of many possible reinforcers in exchange for a token.

USING TOKENS TO
INCENTIVES TO REDUCE ABSENTEEISM

TO REDUCE ABSENTEEISM, a similar program was implemented in a garment factory in Cape Town, South Africa. In the year preceding the program, the average weekly absenteeism rate had been 3.06 percent. As in the Mexico plant, an annual bonus (for fewer than three absences a month) had failed to control the problem. Researchers tested an incentive program with 46 female workers. Half the workers received a weekly bonus for perfect attendance and half did not. A reversal design with two baseline periods and two incentive periods was used.

The incentive program was identical to the Mexican program. Each worker was given a slip of paper (token) indicating that she had earned a small bonus when she arrived at work. The workers were told that the bonus was for coming to work rather than for being on-time. Workers in the control group knew nothing of the program and continued under the annual bonus system. When the incentive program was in effect, the absenteeism rate was considerably lower (2.56%) among workers receiving incentives than among those in the control group (3.70%). It increased again

Both programs demonstrated that reinforcement of arriving at work on time can effectively reduce tardiness and absenteeism. On an ongoing basis, however, these program as they were administered had a common drawback. The desired behavior was reinforced each time it occurred. Although the most rapid change occurs when behavior is continuously reinforced, a continuously reinforced behavior extinguishes rapidly once the reinforcement is discontinued This is exactly what happened in both programs: When the incentives were discontinued, the rate of tardiness and absenteeism returned to its former levels.

REINFORCEMENT MENU

JUST AS THE NAME IMPLIES a reinforcement menu is a list of reinforcers that an employee can choose from. This flexible tool can be used in conjunction with points in implementing a contingency contract. Using the TASC+ coaching model, you and the employee identify several desired reinforcers, assign each a point value, and list them in menu form. When the employee successfully performs the contracted behavior, the points earned are exchanged for one of the reinforcers on the menu. The menu provides an easy method of using variety of reinforcers. Employees can select the most power reinforcers for themselves at that time. In addition, it allows for more than one behavior change program.

Consider the following system worked out between Roger, a management trainee, and Louis, his supervisor. "Roger did quality work, but he also took a lot of breaks and was often late in the morning and after lunch. Louis said, "I met with Roger for a coaching session. We discussed the problem. I expressed my expectations and explored reinforcers. Roger said he was primarily interested in learning the skills necessary to move into management. He said he wanted more direct supervision from me, and that he had a hard time pinning me down. I didn't know this before. He continued to state that he liked to have flexibility in his time. I told him he had to arrive on time in the mornings, and he said that that was a real problem for him. I agreed to help him develop his management skills and suggested that the first area he needed to work on was to contribute more in the staff meetings. Roger agreed but said it was difficult for him to speak out in groups.

R+menus allow for choice.

We carefully pinpointed each behavior expected, set up a point system, and agreed on a menu. Each day Roger was on time in the morning, he received one activity point. For each 15 minutes of task performance he received one point. And for each problem-solving comment he made in the weekly staff meeting he received two activity points."

ROGER'S REWARD MENU

Points	Rewarding Activity
5	Five minutes leisure reading at desk
5	Five-minute break
10	Five minutes added to lunch hours
10	Five minutes off early on Friday
10	Ten minutes reviewing learning tapes
10	Ten minutes studying in library
15	Ten minutes skill supervision (by appointment)
100	One day off for training seminar

Multiple Uses

THIS EXAMPLE ILLUSTRATES how the same point and menu system can be used in several behavior change programs. Louis can assist Roger in increasing on-time behavior, in developing group leader skills, and in managing his on-task time better. The reinforcers were of two kinds, those that allowed for leisure activities and those that encouraged professional growth. The leisure activities were those that Roger was currently enjoying non-contingently and that were causing Louis concern. The opportunity for development was something that Roger had been promised but was not really forthcoming.

By making the expectations and contingencies explicit, Louis was assisted in carrying out his responsibilities to Roger and Roger was confronted with having to assume responsibility for his choices. He could choose an immediate pleasurable activity or he could work toward a desired goal. In the process Roger had an opportunity to improve his self-managing skills.

The effectiveness of the reinforcement menu has been scientifically validated in a variety of educational and therapeutic settings. Little research has been conducted on its use in the organization. Many of the supervisors

Menus can be expanded.

in my workshops, like Louis, have employed variations of the menu with positive results.

When introduced on a department-wide basis, the same point menu can be utilized for all employees, yet each person can have a tailored reinforcement menu. In this way it can simultaneously be used as a corrective device with problem employees and as a maintenance device with those performing on target. After all, if you reserve it only for correcting problem behaviors, you may inadvertently be reinforcing problem behavior. That is, employees who exhibit too many undesirable behaviors or too few desirable ones may be reinforced their undesirable behavior by the special attention and increased reinforcement, whereas those performing satisfactorily receive none. The example with Louis and Roger illustrated how to use reinforcement menus to maintain on-target behavior. Very simply Roger received one point for each 15 minutes of task performance.

Preventative

Used on an ongoing department-wide basis, the menu can be a preventive measure. Consider the new staff member. This person has probably just left an environment that had dramatically different contingencies, and rarely are the daily operating contingencies explain to the new employee. Instead, upon entering your department, the person must decipher the contingencies through an unspoken trial-and-error process. Suppose that in the last position this person was reinforced for autonomous work and independent decision making. Naturally this individual would probably exhibit this behavior in the new environment, your department. But if you prefer to review decisions and monitor work a bit more closely, you may view this employee's behavior as "challenging" and respond negatively, which would probably surprise the new person.

There is no way to predict how such an individual might respond—perhaps even with aggression or withdrawal. At this point it is easy to inadvertently set into motion a negative vicious cycle, one that could have been avoided by having made explicit all your expectations and contingencies. At best there would be a period of confusion and reorganization. The new employee would be experiencing "contingency shock," because several of the contingencies for his or her behavior would have been rearranged suddenly. Obviously, during such an adjustment period, the new person's work efficiency is likely to suffer.

Many of these problems can be prevented by meeting with the new person and setting up a contingency contract implemented by a reinforcement menu. The new person does not have to try to guess your subtle expectations, but during the coaching can express his or her own expectations and desired contingencies. With this approach you can establish-from the very first day-open communication as well as a foundation for resolving problems. It provides a method of emphasizing the interrelationship of management and employee and of demonstrating genuine concern for the new person.

Promotes Communication

ANOTHER ADVANTAGE of using the reinforcement menu on such an ongoing basis is that it provides a means of additional reinforcement. The menu can be expanded, for example. Instead of being allotted on a random and non-contingent basis, privileges can be contingently linked to improved performance. By working out menus with employees, you have the opportunity to expand your own reinforcing repertoire.

Many employees will suggest reinforcers that you may never have considered, but will find acceptable. In the process of negotiating contingencies, employees can be encouraged to question the standards and to provide feedback. Even when they do not agree with the standards, they are more likely to cooperate when they know that their views have been considered. Their feedback also provides an opportunity to reexamine and possibly alter outmoded or unrealistic standards. Finally, having such an ongoing system in effect makes more complex and sophisticated change programs easy to implement.

20

Maintaining Peak Performance

IT IS IMPORTANT TO PLAN AHEAD how to maintain productivity gains otherwise they are likely to decline overtime. Maintaining a behavior at the desired frequency is the final step in the behavior change program. Contingencies that maintain behavior are different from those that promote change.

ALTER THE SCHEDULE OF REINFORCEMENT

ONE MAINTENANCE STRATEGY is stretching out the reinforcement—that is, switching from a continuous schedule in which each incident of the desired behavior is reinforced to an intermittent one where some but not all incidences of the desired behavior are reinforced..

> Continuous reinforcement where each instance of the behavior is reinforced is powerful for *increasing* performance;
>
> Intermittent reinforcement that comes unpredictably is most effective in *maintaining* performance at a high frequency.

Don't make an abrupt switch, however, which would cause contingency shock. Instead slowly stretch or fade out the reinforcement. If a feedback system was used as part of the intervention, continue it into the maintenance phase. Employees can use the feedback to prompt self-reinforcement.

REARRANGE EXISTING CONTINGENCIES

AN ALTERNATIVE MAINTENANCE STRATEGY is to rearrange existing contingencies so that reinforcers already present in the environment are made contingent on the desired behavior. Change programs in which the contingencies were rearranged become self-maintaining as long as the new arrangement of contingencies stays in effect. Suppose, for example, that you want your staff to arrive promptly

Use existing positive contingencies.

at meetings so you rearrange the existing contingencies (waiting or avoiding waiting) by starting on time instead of starting late, so that you reinforce promptness rather than being late. Arriving on time will probably continue as long as the contingencies remain the same—that is, as long as you start the meeting on time.

Natural Reinforcers

SOME CHANGE PROGRAMS have built-in contingencies that reinforce the desired behavior. These programs could be considered self-maintaining. For example, a salesperson's improved sales skills are continually reinforced by increased sales. On the other hand, interventions that involve additional or new reinforcement, building in natural reinforcers becomes an important step. For example, if Arlene's supervisor stops reinforcing her for independent problem solving, Arlene is likely to begin asking for assistance again. Arlene's supervisor needs to develop natural reinforcers as a maintenance procedure.

Natural reinforcers generally fall into two categories: self-reinforcement and reinforcement from others. For example, Arlene's supervisor could encourage Arlene to implement a self-management program to teach herself to use self-reinforcement, such as saying to herself, "I just made a good suggestion!". In addition, the supervisor could encourage others in the work environment to reinforce Arlene's suggestions.

Reinforce the Reinforcer

POSITIVE REMARKS about Arlene's suggestions from her peers could be prompted, such as "Lorrie, what did you think of Arlene's suggestion?" and then reinforced, "I'm glad I asked your opinion, Lorrie, because you made a good point." To do this you simply set up a behavior change program that has as its target behavior increased mutual reinforcement among peers. Collect baseline data on your staff and use appropriately applied contingent reinforcement. Monitor the frequency of peers' mutual reinforcement.

Reinforcing the reinforcer builds a team.

This barometer reveals the cohesiveness of your team. Reinforcing the reinforcer is an important technique for building a team. As the team's cohesiveness grows, demands on you are reduced because the team maintains itself and can actually energize you.

Build In Stimulus Control

Wʜᴇɴᴇᴠᴇʀ ᴘᴏssɪʙʟᴇ, build stimulus control—powerful cues to prompt performance—into your program. Arrange for antecedents in the environment to prompt the behavior. Reinforce peers for prompting one another, and don't let the antecedent become contaminated. If you want the office to retain stimulus control over work behavior, make sure that socializing occurs only in the social area and not in the work area.

Clearly defined rules and limits adhered to fairly and consistently maintain stimulus control. "Smoking is permitted in the social area only and never by anyone in the stockroom" is a statement of stimulus control. Rules do not have to be rigid, but they must be consistent. And it is the consequences of rule-following or rule-breaking that reveal consistency. Rules and norms can maintain work-oriented interactions. "People work together around here." This creates an expectation. If cooperative work is subsequently reinforced, the expectation can become a maintaining antecedent. In a similar manner, goals can maintain high productivity. Goals become a maintaining antecedent when goal attainment is consistently reinforced.

EVALUATION

Eᴠᴀʟᴜᴀᴛɪᴏɴ ɪs ᴀɴ ᴏɴɢᴏɪɴɢ ᴘʀᴏᴄᴇss, not a separate activity that occurs after the termination of the plan; it. Through constant monitoring and counting, current behavior frequencies are compared with the baseline. As long as the desired behavior is steadily increasing, continue your intervention. When the behavior being shaped plateaus or drops in frequency, critically review

Evaluation is ongoing.

and revise your intervention. For example, by charting Otto's behavior, Georgia can easily evaluate her intervention. Because the frequency of Otto's negative comments about the program dropped, she concluded that her intervention was successful.

Careful evaluation can be a tool for recognizing the individuality of your employees. Management strategies presented in books such as this one or in seminars and workshops are general prescriptions and provide general guidelines. But each employee is an individual who has a unique learning history. Thus, change programs that were effective with loggers or bakery workers may not be effective with your employees. Likewise, an approach that works with employees in general may not be effective with a particular employee.

Program evaluation is useful in many ways—most obviously by providing information about the effectiveness of your change program. This is vital in determining whether or not to continue the program. Positive results can help you persuade top management to provide funds and support for implementing your program on a broader basis. In addition, program evaluation provides concrete evidence of your managerial skills. Even when results are not as positive as you might have wanted them to be, merely having conducted systematic evaluation demonstrates that you have essential managerial skills, such as planning and decision making. Publishing the results of your evaluations in in-house publications and trade journals will give others the opportunity to profit from your activities. Colleagues within your company can make use of tactics that you found effective. In the long run, this will help your company because others will not have to rediscover what you have discovered.

CONCLUSION

BEHAVIOR CHANGE PROGRAMS can improve employee productivity. A key agent of change in all organizations at all levels is the immediate supervisor. With behavior management techniques, supervisors can increase employees' performance by teaching them how to work. Few schools teach people how to work; most people learn on the job. Goal setting, self-reinforcement, self-monitoring, developing contingencies, and doing the least-liked work first are work behaviors. Learning by doing is a powerful and efficient educational process. Employees learn to come to work on time by coming to work on time and they learn to set goals by setting goals.

The challenge to the manager is to arrange the work environment so that employees are likely to do their best work.

With tardiness, the supervisor might add a contingent incentive; with goal-setting, the supervisor might guide the subordinate through the process many times. Learning to work is a continuous process: Accomplishing the objectives of one change program sets the stage for the next one. Once employees learn to be on time for an immediate continuous payoff, for example, they need to learn to continue to arrive on time for a less frequent payoff. The first intervention might involve receiving an incentive every time the employee is on time; the second might use intermittent incentives and goal-setting. Managers are in a key position-they can facilitate or inhibit the performance of those they supervise. And by learning to use the skills and techniques outlined in this book, they can become agents of change-and teachers.

Learning to work is a continuous process.

Index

U

V

W

Docpotter Library

Overcoming Job Burnout
How to Renew Enthusiasm for Work

Dr. Beverly Potter,
Illustrations by Phil Frank

ISBN 1-57951-000-0
$14.95   310 pg.

Tens of millions of workers in the United States suffer from feelings of powerlessness in the workplace which can destroy motivation and enthusiasm for work. Burnout is especially prevalent in this era of restructuring and job displacement.

Overcoming Job Burnout tells how to renew enthusiasm for work by developing personal power. This upbeat guide shows how to recognize job burnout and overcome it through a progression of positive changes, including setting goals, managing stress, building a strong social support system, modifying the job, developing needed skills, changing jobs, modifying powerless thinking and developing detached concern.

Provides important information that managers, counselors, and individuals can utilize daily to eliminate feelings of powerlessness on the job and includes the *Burnout Potential Inventory, Am I Burning Out?* and *Is My Staff Burning Out?* tests. Illustrations, index.

ISBN for new edition:1-57951-074-4

Preventing
Job Burnout
A Workbook
Dr. Beverly Potter

ISBN 1-56052-357-3
$10.95   112 pg.

Hands-on guide, filled with fun-to-do exercises. This makes a great text for workshops. Good for anyone who really wants specific techniques to tackle their job doledrums and renew their enthusiasm for working.

Beating Job Burnout
How to Increase
Job Satisfaction
Dr. Beverly Potter

ISBN 0-914171-41-0
$9.95   1 hour audio cassette

A lively and informative *Psychology Today* interview with Docpotter. Describes the symptoms and causes of job burnout and how to overcome it. Great listening during commute time.

Finding a Path with a Heart
How to Go from Burnout to Bliss

Dr. Beverly Potter,
Foreword by Michael Toms,
Illustrations by Phil Frank
ISBN 0-914171-74-7
$14.95   356 pg.

Finding a Path with a Heart shows how to find direction and meaning in your work and your life by finding your own path, one that is in tune with your values, one that will make your heart sing. In this work Docpotter offers a step-by-step method for becoming a "self-leader"—so that you can set your direction and have a joyous journey. Illustrations, charts, index.

Fascinating, useful and enjoyable to read. —NAPRA Review

From Conflict to Cooperation
How to Mediate a Dispute

Dr. Beverly Potter,
Illustrations by Phil Frank
ISBN 0-914171-79-8
$14.95   194 pg.

Techniques for mediators to resolve disputes. This manual shows how to intervene to control hostility while uncovering each party's perspective on the issues involved. It then demonstrates how to mediate an agreement.

Superb guide to mediating disputes...excellent source...

a basic training manual for those involved in mediating disputes.

Potter's handbook is highly recommended.—Library Journal

Get Peak Performance Everyday

How to Manage Like a Coach

Dr. Beverly Potter
ISBH 1-57951-063-9 $12.95   192 pg.
How to use scientific principles to manage people at work more effectively. When people are poorly managed, work is hell, employees burnout, and productivity takes a nose-dive. But when people are managed skillfully, working is stimulating, employees gain a sense of control and pride, peak performance is a daily event and productivity soars.

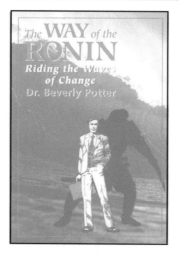

The Way of the Ronin
Riding the Waves of Change at Work

Dr. Beverly Potter
Foreword by Dennis Jaffe, PhD
ISBN 1-57951-051-5
$14.95   192 pg.

The ronin career strategy is based on versatility, independence, initiative and savvy. Rather than focusing on a narrow career path, ronin surf the waves of change by building a wide range of skills and using work as an adventure. An inspiring alternative to the ladder-climbing mentality of the corporate world. Strategies to escape from "corporate feudalism" to establish yourself on the cutting edge.

An intelligent and inspiring book. —ALA Booklist

Selected as a "recommended business book." —Library Journal

Maverick As Master in the Marketplace
The Way of the Office Warrior

Dr. Beverly Potter
ISBN 0-914171-42-9
$9.95   1 hour audio cassette

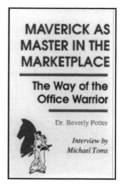

Interview with Michael Toms of New Dimensions Radio provides insights to empower the independent minded to rise above corporate feudalism and get ahead while enjoying it more.

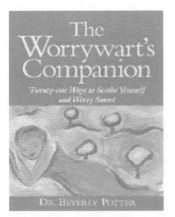

The Worrywart's Companion

Twenty-One Ways to Soothe Yourself & Worry Smart

Dr. Beverly Potter
ISBN 1-885171-15-3
$12.95 192 pg

Worry is a kind of mental fire-drill, but worrywarts get fixated on their fears of catastrophe and drive themselves—and everyone around them—nuts! Learn how to shake the worrywart habit to "worry smart"— worry that actually helps to improve your life and keep you safe. Fun to read and filled with good advice.

DRUG TESTING AT WORK

A Guide for Employers

Beverly A. Potter, PhD, & J. Sebastian Orfali, MA
ISBN 1-57951-07-8
$24.95   279 pg.-5
Describes the tests and how they work, discusses the civil rights issues and tells how to set up a drug testing program. It tells employers how to reduce exposure to lawsuits and reveals how employees beat the test. It includes a chart of drug detection periods, how to flush drugs out of the body, how to adulterate and substitute samples and how to foil the paperwork.

Pass the Test
An Employee Guide to Drug Testing

Beverly A. Potter, PhD, & J. Sebastian Orfali, M.A.
ISBN 1-57951-008-6
$16.95   160 pg.
How tests work, legal rights as an employee, and what you can do to make sure your employer tests fairly. What over-the-counter medicines and foods, like poppy seeds, can cause false results. What steps to take to pass the test. Written for the millions of people in corporate America who don't abuse drugs.

Brain Boosters
Foods & Drugs that Make You Smarter

Beverly Potter, PhD & Sebastian Orfali, MA
ISBN 0-914171-65-8
$16.95   256 pg
Comprehensive guide to smart drugs and nutrients. How the brain works and the factors influencing mental performance, tells about the evolution and growing use of nutrients and pharmaceuticals to improve brain function, from patients and cyberpunks to the mainstream. Includes a laymen's description of the most important pharmaceuticals, vitamins, nutrients and herbs used to boost brain power. Charts. List of doctors.

The Healing Magic of Cannabis
It's the High that Heals!

Dr. Beverly Potter
Dan Joy
ISBN 1-57951-001-9
$14.95 192 pg
Cannabis eases tension, reduces stress, triggers the relaxation response, and fosters optimistic thinking and positive mental attitudes. How the psychoactivity of cannabis relates to the mind's role in physical healing.

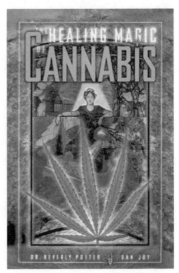

High Performance Goal Setting
Using Intuition to Conceive & Achieve Your Dreams

Dr. Beverly Potter
ISBN1-57951-012-4
$9.95   96 pg
Intuition is the "secret weapon" of high performers. High performance goals are powerful—compelling and magnetic so they pull you towards the goal the way a magnet would, so that you don't have to drive yourself. Filled with interesting illustrtions, set in easy to read large type, making it a quick read that in fun and pops right into your head. Easy to implement techniques and charming "Shaman Woman" stories characteristic of Docpotter's work.

This is definitely a book for "the rest of us. —NAPRA Review

ABOUT DOCPOTTER

Dr. Beverly Potter's work blends the philosophies of humanistic psychology and Eastern mysticism with principles of behavior modification to create an inspiring approach to handling the many challenges encountered in today's workplace.

Docpotter earned her masters of science in vocational rehabilitation counseling from San Francisco State and her doctorate in counseling psychology form Stanford University. She was a member of the Stanford Staff Development team for 18 years, has taught in a variety of postgraduate programs and is a dynamic and informative speaker. Her workshops have been sponsored by numerous colleges, corporations, associations and governmental agencies. She has authored many books and is best known for her work on overcoming job burnout.

Docpotter's website is docpotter.com and is loaded with useful informaiton. Please visit.